The Bread Machine Magic Book of Helpful Hints

(Second Revised Edition)

Also by Linda Rehberg and Lois Conway

Bread Machine Magic
More Bread Machine Magic

The Bread Machine Magic Book of Helpful Hints

(Second Revised Edition)

Dozens of Problem-solving Hints and
Troubleshooting Techniques for
Getting the Most Out of Your Bread Machine

INCLUDES 55 RECIPES

LINDA REHBERG AND LOIS CONWAY

Illustrations by Durell Godfrey

St. Martin's Griffin
New York

This book is dedicated to Dennis and Jim,
two wonderful men who were born with twinkles in their eyes,
an Irish song in their souls, and
hearts quick and strong in their generous impulses.

"May the rocks in your field turn to gold."
—an old Irish toast

THE BREAD MACHINE MAGIC BOOK OF HELPFUL HINTS (SECOND REVISED EDITION). Copyright ©
1999, 1995, 1993 by Linda Rehberg and Lois Conway. Illustrations copyright © 1993 by Durell
Godfrey. All rights reserved. Printed in the United States of America. No part of this book
may be used or reproduced in any manner whatsoever without written permission
except in the case of brief quotations embodied in critical articles or reviews.
For information address St. Martin's Press, 175 Fifth Avenue, New York, N.Y. 10010.

Library of Congress Cataloging-in-Publication Data

Rehberg, Linda.
The bread machine magic book of helpful hints : dozens of problem-
solving hints and troubleshooting techniques for getting the most
out of your bread machine : includes 55 recipes / Linda Rehberg and
Lois Conway : illustrations by Durell Godfrey. —2nd rev. ed.
          p.   cm.
"Second St. Martin's Griffin ed." —T.p. verso.
Includes index.
ISBN 0-312-24123-2
1. Automatic bread machines.   I. Conway, Lois.   II. Title.
TX769.R383   1999
641.8′15—dc21   99-36687
                              CIP

Second St. Martin's Griffin Edition: November 1999

10 9 8 7 6 5 4 3 2 1

Contents

Acknowledgments

Looking at the acknowledgment page in our last book, *Bread Machine Magic,* you would have thought we'd written The Great American Novel! We will try to contain ourselves this time. There are, however, many wonderful people who are a major part of this book. Most of them are former Prodigy members who have taken us many, many more steps down this road then we ever thought we'd travel. We hope that when you read this book you'll see how much their spirits are a part of it. We wish to acknowledge and thank Irwin Franzel, our favorite rocket scientist, "Zoji" bread baker, and friend. The depth of his knowledge, his willingness to respond to a daily barrage of questions, and his compassion for other human beings was limitless. Linda Caldwell is another kindhearted human being whom we've loved from the day she threatened to do a song-and-dance routine in her tap shoes and Groucho glasses at our first cooking class. Her charming personality radiates right through the video screen and she is always the first to lend a hand on the bulletin board when someone's having bread machine problems. We also send our many thanks to both Gene Hill and Melody Gabriel, who took so much time to answer all our questions on gluten-free breads and shared their favorite recipes with us. We've been very fortunate to meet and become friends with people like Susan Lipton, Diana Lewis, Christiane Stakely, Marianne Wright, and Michelle Cook. In addition to their many witty and humorous notes, they all shared helpful hints that were incorporated into this book. Many people passed through Prodigy's revolving door, shared their experiences, gave us valuable feedback, expanded our knowledge, and kept us on our toes. We wish to say "thank you" to all of you.

We are very much indebted to Glenna Vance, who, on her own time, spent many hours running nutritional analyses of all our recipes.

Once again, we never would have made it through without Debbie and Rick Carlson's computer wisdom and patience in times of extreme stress to keep us up and running. Thank you both!

Ann Slaybaugh, Jim Bodle, and Dawn Fletcher . . . thanks for sharing and inspiring some great recipes!

We would also like to thank Ann Slaybaugh and Scott Parker, two very special teachers at Poway High School, for lending a hand with the math problems. Linda would still be trying to figure out those substitutions if it weren't for you!

Jana Cason, we are very grateful to you for nursing us along in our fledgling teaching careers. Your wonderful sense of humor, gentle guidance, and kind support meant a lot to us.

Barbara Anderson, our editor for the original version, still holds a special place in our hearts. Her calm, soothing voice over the phone was music to our ears in times of panic. We will always be grateful for her insightful comments, direction, and unwavering support. Marian Lizzi stepped in to fill the void Barbara left and we were delighted to find we were still in very competent hands. Marian, you've been the very essence of patience and we thank you for making this revised edition possible.

There were lots of friends, co-workers, and neighbors who helped us out a great deal by taking all this bread off our hands. We always appreciated your comments and hope you'll be nearby when we start testing recipes for the next book.

Thank you, Shayna, for the impact your nature-loving, animal-preserving lifestyle has had on us. We're certain you'll contribute much more than Vegan Burgers to this world in your lifetime.

This certainly wouldn't be complete without mentioning the family pets . . . four very special testers: Peppy Rehberg and the Conway brood of Soft Coated Wheaten Terriers—Briscoe, Missy, and Susie. Theirs are discriminating palates indeed.

Our love and our gratitude are strongest felt for the two men in our lives, Jim and Dennis. Once again they endured countless nights without dinners, testy wives, kitchens torn up or turned into laboratories, and nonexistent social lives. The dust has settled, and it's great to see you're both still here.

Introduction

The love affair continues. . . .

When we finished our first book, *Bread Machine Magic*, we thought our bread machine "career" was over. We moved all but our favorite machines to the garage, took a deep breath, and contemplated the many ways we would take some time off to kick back and relax. But what we discovered was that our first book was only the beginning. We were immediately caught up in a flurry of activities. We did numerous book signings, joined the Prodigy network, began teaching bread machine classes, and answered hundreds of phone calls and letters. Everyone had questions, questions, questions, and we didn't always have the answers! We had to pull out those dusty bread machines and go back to work. If we didn't find the answers in the kitchen, we headed for our local libraries. We attended cooking classes. It was obvious that our wonderful relationship with the bread machine wasn't over. It was simply blossoming into a new dimension.

We met, spoke, and communicated with hundreds of determined yet frustrated bread machine owners. At book signings and classes, strangers hugged and thanked us when we came up with solutions to their common problems. (We'll work for hugs any day!) Those who had purchased a bread machine because they didn't know the first thing about baking seemed to be in need of basic information. The experienced bakers threw more difficult questions our way and always asked "Why?" It was in the middle of a book signing that the idea for this book finally bubbled to the surface. Though people encouraged us to write another cookbook, it was obvious that what they truly needed was the information we were teaching in our classes!

We scooped up all our teaching notes, jotted down the questions people asked, conducted endless tests, and at night fell asleep reading dozens of books to expand our basic understanding of the science and inexact art of baking bread. For several months, Linda typed morning, noon, and night, while Lois worked the phones.

Our sights were set on combining all we possibly could into one unique book, a handy reference guide for bread machine owners. People with special dietary needs constantly wanted to know how to eliminate or lower the fat, sugar, cholesterol, sodium, or animal products in their breads. "How does one adjust to adverse weather conditions or high-altitude baking?" people asked. Our favorite was the woman who wanted to know how to lighten up her breads. She claimed her breads were so dense and heavy that when the birds ate them, they fell out of the sky! We were asked if it was possible to bake breads in the machine free of wheat or gluten. We've answered these concerns to the best of our ability. It's our hope that you'll find this book a very useful kitchen companion and a helping hand. Baking home-made bread is meant to be a very simple pleasure. We wish that for you most of all.

Your questions spurred us on, kept us on our toes, and inspired this book. We feel much of it was written, in a sense, by all of you. Therefore, we'd like to end this introduction to your book with a few of our favorite quotes from the bread machine bakers on the Prodigy network. People like this are why we still have an ongoing love affair with bread machines and the wonderful people who use them.

"My advice is to accept your current inabilities and bake, bake, bake. Every loaf I made was a learning experience in itself. Experiment and get the feel of the flours, the dough, and use as many senses as possible to learn to make the type of bread dearest to your heart."

—BENJAMIN PRATER

"The automatic bread machine is an example of using high tech to restore us to one of the simple pleasures of childhood. In honor of this paradox, I keep the bread machine sitting on top of an ancient food-treadle sewing machine."

—GINNIE SAMS

"Bread touches a heartstring in our souls that reminds us of cold days and the warmth of a mother's touch and snuggling in close to the hearth."

—KAREN DAY

I
Bread Machines

THE VARIOUS BREAD MACHINE FEATURES

The two questions we're asked most often are: "Which bread machine is your favorite?" and "Which machine do you recommend I buy?" While we're more than happy to rave about our favorites and can recommend several, they're our favorites because they suit *our* needs. It's far better if we help educate you about all the available features so that in the end the machine you take home will be one in your price range with features that *you*—not we—feel are essential.

So, if you're an undecided prospective bread machine owner, befuddled by the multitude of options bread machines offer, read on. What follows is a description of the various bread machine features now available. If you check off the options you most desire, you can approach the business of selecting a new bread machine with confidence. You will be an informed buyer.

You can also use the Internet as a resource. (Start with our Web site at *www.breadmachinemagic.com* and follow the links or try the *rec.food.baking* and *rec.food.equipment* news group.) One word of caution: Take in all recommendations with the understanding that almost every bread machine owner loves his or her particular brand and highly recommends it over all others. There are many, many good ones on the market now but it's unwise to select a machine based solely on a few recommendations from people you don't know. Pay more heed to those having problems with a particular model or brand.

PRICE

For the most part, bread machines range in price from $99 up to $250. As with everything else in life, you get what you pay for. We encourage you to not make your selection based on price alone. Always take the features the machine offers into consideration, too. If money is a concern, look for sales on the more expensive machines. Shop discount stores. Purchase through catalogues such as *The Wholesale-by-Mail Catalogue* by Lowell Miller and Prudence McCullough (New York: Harper Collins Publishers, 1992), which is updated regularly. We urge you to buy the very best machine you can afford.

LOAF SIZE

These days, most bread machines are sold as 1½- or 2-pound size machines (though that's just a rough estimate of the weight of the breads they produce). The 1½-pound loaf calls for about 3 cups flour. The 2-pound loaf uses 4 cups flour.

The benefit of buying the larger 2-pound machine with a vertical pan is that you have the option of making small, medium, or large loaves as desired. The small 1-pound loaves (2 cups flour) are the perfect size for one or two people. Since homemade breads contain no artificial preservatives, they usually remain fresh for only two or three days. You're better off making smaller, fresh loaves more often than baking a large loaf that takes a week to consume. It gives you the opportunity for more variety, too.

LOAF SHAPE

Most machines produce a rectangular loaf of bread in a horizontal or a vertical bread pan. There are advantages to both types of pan. The horizontal pan produces the more attractive bread, one that resembles in appearance a homemade bread baked in the oven. It's perfect for gift giving. If it weren't for the telltale hole in the bottom, no one would ever know it was baked in a machine. The vertical pan is more versatile. Because the bread is turned on its side and sliced, every slice is consistently the same size square. If your bread doesn't rise very tall one time or hits the lid the next time, you'll still have the same size slice of bread, just fewer or more of them, whichever the case may be. For that reason, too, only the vertical pan allows you to bake the loaf size of your choice—small, medium, or large.

PREHEAT CYCLE

Some machines will warm the ingredients either prior to mixing or during the kneading phase. There's no need to warm your ingredients to room temperature if your machine does it for you. At first we liked this feature. It seemed to ensure consistently good results, and back in those days, preheating only lasted about 5 minutes. Unfortunately, now it's more of an annoyance than a benefit. In newer machines the preheat cycle can be as much as 40 minutes long! That means 40 minutes before mixing ever begins. Since the most crucial step in producing good bread is to judge the consistency of the dough as it mixes, having to wait 30 or 40 minutes to do so is intolerable. With that long a delay, we'd like to see the manufacturers include a way to skip the preheat cycle when desired. Ask to see the instruction booklet when shopping for a bread machine. Most have a diagram of the cycles and their lengths. Be sure to note how long the preheat cycle is, if there is one.

RAPID BAKE CYCLE

This cycle bakes bread approximately 1 hour faster than the Standard Bake Cycle. It's also referred to as a Quick Bake or Turbo cycle. The duration of the Standard Bake cycle varies widely from machine to machine; some are 3½ to 4 hours, others are as short as 1 hour! Therefore, some bread machines list no Rapid Bake cycle but their Standard Bake cycle may actually be a Rapid Bake (which we consider to be anything under 3 hours). Refer to the instruction booklet for the length of the various baking cycles.

With the frantic pace of our lives, the speediness of an appliance is certainly a key selling point, but in the case of homemade bread, you need to weigh speed versus flavor. That wonderful flavor you so cherish in homemade bread can only be developed over time. A rapidly produced bread will be good but it just won't have the same body and aroma. However, if baking bread always seems to be a last-minute activity for you, then the rapid baking machines are your answer.

DOUGH (OR MANUAL) CYCLE

This feature signals you to remove the dough at the stage where it's ready to be shaped, allowed to rise one last time, and then baked. Every machine has this option, and even if you're not a hands-on bread baker at this point, you'll learn to enjoy this feature in time. We've nicknamed it the "Fun Cycle." You can use it for something as simple as making your own hamburger buns or tackle something more creative by braiding a beautiful Challah bread for Rosh Hashanah. If you're looking for a show stopper, create a cornucopia made from dough and then fill it with homemade rolls for Thanksgiving. (You'll find recipes for the Challah and the cornucopia in our book *More Bread Machine Magic.*)

WHOLE WHEAT CYCLE

This cycle extends the kneading and rising phases, which is a boon for breads that contain at least 50 percent whole-grain flours. Can you bake whole-grain breads in machines without this feature? Yes. Without the extended cycles, however, sometimes you need to compensate by adjusting your ingredients, adding gluten, or stopping and restarting your machine after the first kneading cycle—all in an effort to achieve taller, lighter, whole-grain loaves.

FRENCH BREAD CYCLE

This cycle is best suited for breads low in fat and sugar. Usually, less time is spent kneading the dough and more time is devoted to the rising cycle, which results in breads with crisp, crackly crusts and coarse, chewy interiors. You can produce crisp-crusted breads in machines that do not have this feature by eliminating the fat and reducing the sugar in your recipes. Such loaves won't be identical to those baked on a French cycle, however.

SWEET BREAD CYCLE

Some machines offer this feature in addition to offering a crust color selector. It's best suited for breads that are high in sugar or fat (more than 2 tablespoons) or breads that burn easily, such as egg, cheese, and some whole-grain breads. In most cases, your bread will bake at a lower temperature. In other machines, it's also a longer cycle, start-to-finish, than the standard cycle.

RAISIN/NUT CYCLE

This feature comes in handy when you want to bake a bread with raisins, chopped dried fruits, or nuts. The machine will signal late in the kneading phase when it's time to add those extras. It prevents them from being pulverized, which can happen if they're added in the very beginning with the rest of the ingredients. If the machine you purchased doesn't have this feature, you can set a timer to ring about 5 to 10 minutes before the end of the final kneading cycle to alert you that it's time to add the extras.

JAM/BUTTER/CAKES/QUICK BREADS

These are options available on the "deluxe" machines. Some people dismiss them at first, but once they stop and think about slathering a thick slice of warm, fresh-baked bread with some delicious homemade jam or butter, this feature becomes much more enticing!

Quick breads (not to be confused with breads baked on a Rapid Bake cycle) are non-yeast breads such as banana nut bread, pumpkin bread, etc. You can also bake small cakes using the Quick Bread cycle.

Cool-Down/Keep-Warm Cycle

Though it won't cool the bread completely after baking, the ½-hour Cool-Down cycle will remove excessive heat and moisture from the machine so you won't be left with a soggy, limp loaf in case you're not around when the baking ends.

Instead of cooling the finished bread, some machines have a Keep-Warm cycle that does the opposite. It keeps the bread warm for several hours until you're able to remove it from the machine.

Delayed Bake Timer

Undoubtedly, this is the most popular bread machine feature of all. It allows you to program your machine to bake at a specified time, which means you can wake to the heady aroma of freshly baked bread (could there be a better alarm clock?) or be greeted by an intoxicating fragrance after a hard day at work. For that reason, this feature is standard on every machine.

Delayed Bake Timer for the Dough Cycle

Those of us with a passion for pizza and dinner rolls love this cycle. You can place the ingredients in the machine in the morning and have dough ready to use when you walk through the door in the evening. Unfortunately, not many machines have this feature, yet, so read the instruction manuals carefully if you're looking for one that does.

Viewing Window

We've baked thousands of loaves and we still like to "sneak a peek." Actually, the window isn't the frill it might seem to be at first. The best thing you can do to ensure a successful loaf of bread is to check the dough as it kneads. If it appears too wet or too dry, you can make adjustments and avoid disappointing results 4 hours later. It also enables you to spot the dough that is threatening to overflow the bread pan the moment the baking cycle kicks on. (A mere prick with a toothpick will prevent certain disaster.)

Our last, rarely mentioned benefit of the viewing window is that it's a dandy way to entertain children and visiting grandchildren! Pull up a chair so they can peek in and it will fascinate them for quite a while.

CRUST COLOR SELECTION

This is a useful feature when baking breads that are high in sugar or fat, or breads containing cheese, eggs, and whole grains. With a medium crust color setting, they'd bake up too dark. Being able to adjust to a light crust setting is requisite. You'll find this feature on most machines nowadays.

CUSTOM CONTROLS/EXTENDED RISE/PAUSE CYCLE

There are a few machines that allow you to program the cycles from start to finish, jump from one cycle to another, extend the rising time, or pause in mid-rise to fill or coat a dough. Much as that sounds like something only an advanced bread machine baker would use, once you're familiar with your machine, these features are relatively easy to use. It's surprising how many times we've relied on them to give a reluctant riser a little more time or skip ahead to the bake cycle when a bread is rising too quickly or to remove a dough and coat it with seeds. They're really bonus features worth serious consideration.

POWER SAVER

If you live in an area that experiences frequent power outages, this feature may be your savior. If you electricity goes off or someone pulls the plug, all is not lost. If power is restored within 10 minutes, your machine will start up right where it left off. (If not, simply remove the dough, place it in a greased 8x4-inch (small loaf), 9x5-inch (medium loaf) or two 8x4-inch (large loaf) bread pan(s), allow it to rise until doubled, then bake "the old-fashioned way."

YEAST DISPENSER

Some Panasonic machines have a small compartment in the lid that dispenses the yeast shortly before the second kneading phase rather than adding it in the beginning with the rest of the ingredients. The yeast dispenser guarantees that the yeast will remain dry and not activate prematurely when using the Delayed Bake setting. Since the yeast is separated from the rest of the ingredients, the machine is able to mix the yeast-free dough the moment you press Start, even on the Delayed Timer. This unique feature enables you to judge and make adjustments to *all* bread doughs immediately.

MISCELLANEOUS

Other features to consider, which may or may not be important to you:

· A removable lid makes cleanup easier.

· The size of the machine can be a consideration if you're short on counter space.

· If you simply don't have room for another appliance on your countertop, know that there are now combination toaster oven/bread machines being produced.

· Some control panels are difficult to read at counter height. Make sure the machine you're considering has a readable one.

SERVICING

When selecting a machine, it's also important to keep in mind the servicing aspect. Most machines are real workhorses and rarely develop mechanical problems, but when they do, the quality of the manufacturer's customer service becomes vitally important. You don't want to be told it will be three months before they can repair/replace your machine. It pays to ask other bread machine owners what their experiences with customer service have been. The good news is, most manufacturers work very hard to keep the customer satisfied. Some of the nicest people you'll ever want to meet work in this industry.

Also, if you have a local appliance repair shop that handles bread machines, ask questions about the problems they see most often and their opinion of the machine(s) you're considering purchasing. They're the ones who know these machines inside and out.

2
Bread-baking Facts and Guidelines

The Science and Art of Baking Bread

We think it would be useful to share a few facts about bread baking in general. For those of you who have never baked a loaf of bread by hand, we'd like to give you a better understanding of some of the elements involved in producing that "mini-miracle" each time you press the Start button. For those of you who are experienced bread bakers, we hope we've done our research well enough to surprise you with one or two new facts.

The Essential Ingredients

· Gluten, the protein found mainly in wheat flour, gives bread its structure. The higher the gluten content, the higher and stronger the loaf will be.

· Yeast, a living organism, is activated when it comes in contact with warm liquids. It feeds on sugars and produces bubbles of carbon dioxide gas, which cause the bread to slowly rise.

· Flour contains gluten, starch, and enzymes that can convert the starch into sugar.

· Liquids activate the yeast and bind the dough.

· Salt moderates the yeast's activity and strengthens the gluten structure.

Mixing/Kneading the Dough

· As the dough is mixed and later kneaded, the tangled elastic strands of gluten in the flour begin to unfold and form a weblike structure. (If you take a well-kneaded piece of dough, roll it out very thin, and hold it up to the light, you can easily see the gluten structure.)

· At the same time malt enzymes, found in both wheat flour and barley, begin to break down the starch molecules in the flour(s) and turn them into sugars . . . food for the yeast.

· The amount and type of kneading largely determines the final texture of the bread. The more you knead the dough (up to a point), the finer the texture will be. As you knead, you break up the little pockets of air being incorporated into the dough. It's these air pockets between the strands of gluten that fill up with the carbon dioxide produced by the yeast. The smaller the air pockets, the finer the bread's texture.

· It is possible to "overknead" bread dough . . . usually by machine, rarely by hand. Its structure will break down, the gluten will lose its elasticity, and you'll be left with a useless, sticky blob of dough. If you stopped and restarted your machine several times after each kneading cycle, you'd risk this happening to your dough.

· When kneading dough by hand, always work in any extra flour a little at a time. Avoid adding large quantities of flour to your dough all at once; you'll end up with a very tough, dry, heavy loaf of bread.

· Well-kneaded dough is smooth and satiny and has a soft, pliable body to it. You should be able to knead it with one hand at that point.

RISING OF THE DOUGH

· Once the dough has been fully kneaded by hand, it is covered and set in a warm location to rise. The dough will eventually double in size.

· As the dough sits, the yeast cells feed on the available sugars, multiply, and produce carbon dioxide gas and alcohol. (That's the fermentation process in a nutshell.) The ever-increasing bubbles of carbon dioxide fill up the open spaces between the weblike strands of gluten, causing the dough to expand and rise.

· The optimum rising temperature is between 80° and 85°F.

· If a dough is "forced" to rise faster by subjecting it to higher temperatures, it will also produce more alcohol, giving the bread a sour taste and unpleasant smell.

· To warm the oven slightly for rising, turn the oven on "warm" for 1 minute, then turn it off, and place the covered dough in the oven to rise until doubled.

· After the first rising, the bread is punched down and usually allowed to rise a second time. Since the yeast organisms have multiplied greatly in number, the loaf will double in size again in about half the time it took to do so the first time.

· Punching down the dough (deflating it gently with your fist) redistributes the yeast and provides it with more oxygen and new food sources. It also forces out some of the excess carbon dioxide and alcohol.

· After the second rising, the dough is turned out onto a floured or lightly oiled countertop, then gently shaped (to avoid breaking gluten strands), placed into bread pans, covered, and left to rise one last time.

· When shaping the dough into braids, dinner rolls, pizza crusts, etc., it's easier to handle if you first place it on a lightly floured surface, cover it, and allow it to rest for 10 to 15 minutes. The elastic gluten strands in the dough will relax and it will be much easier to handle. If you've ever struggled with a pizza dough that kept shrinking up every time you tried to stretch it out to the edges of the pan, try letting the dough rest and relax before shaping it to fit the pan. As our friend Jana Cason explains, it's just too "excited"! Also, try to avoid overhandling or adding more flour to the dough at this point. Overhandling and excess flour result in a very inflexible dough and a heavy, tough bread.

· The maximum number of risings is four or five; after that the yeast's food supply is exhausted.

· Breads containing acidic ingredients such as buttermilk, yogurt, sour cream, and lemon juice will rise faster than breads without these ingredients.

· The more you load breads down with heavy ingredients such as fruits and nuts, the slower they will rise.

· Whole-grain bread doughs and other doughs low in gluten need longer kneading times and are slow risers.

· The dough should not expand to more than double its size during the last rise. That leaves a little growing room for the "oven spring"—the yeast's grand finale.

· If the shaped loaves are allowed to "over-rise" to their maximum expansion before baking, oven spring will not occur. Instead, the gas cells will burst, the gluten structure will give way, and the loaves will collapse.

· It's fairly easy to spot over-risen doughs. They are very light, puffy, and have very little body. Rather than bake them and have disappointing results, simply reshape, let rise (watch them carefully this time), and then bake.

BAKING

· There is a wide assortment of baking pans that can be used when baking breads in the oven. If you choose to use a glass or black steel pan, reduce the recommended oven temperature by 25°F to avoid overbrowning the bread. Black pans produce dark-crusted breads, silver pans produce light-crusted breads. If you bake freeform loaves, choose a sturdy stainless-steel baking sheet. There are also special curved French bread pans that will hold two loaves. They are perforated along the bottom to produce crisp crusts. Pizza and baking stones also produce very crisp crusts. Follow the manufacturer's instructions very carefully—they crack if not handled properly. We're read recipes for breads baked in coffee cans, flower pots, on quarry tiles, etc. We caution you to use containers specifically designed for food use to avoid contaminating your breads with toxic materials.

· When the bread is put into the hot oven, the heat causes one last surge in the yeast's activity. More carbon dioxide is created, the gas expands quickly, and there is a rapid increase in the loaf's size. This is called "oven spring."

· Once the interior of the bread reaches 140°F, the yeast dies and the leavening gasses and alcohol evaporate.

· A light-colored loaf will be less flavorful than a dark one.

· Brushing or spraying loaves with water during baking will produce a crisp crust. Loaves brushed with an egg wash before baking will have a shiny, golden crust. Milk brushed on a loaf prior to baking will give it a glossy, dark brown finish. For a soft, tender crust, brush the bread with butter or margarine right after removing it from the oven.

· A perfectly baked loaf of bread is golden brown, nicely rounded on top, hollow sounding when tapped on the bottom, and firm to the touch. It shouldn't be split around the edges, sunken in the middle, or oddly shaped. When the bread has been allowed to cool and then sliced, the interior should reveal a fine crumb with no large air tunnels. Each slice should have a firm body to it and the air pockets should be tiny and uniform in size. If the slice is coarse and full of large holes, very dry and crumbly, or limp, it will be difficult to butter or use in a sandwich.

· Remove bread from pan promptly after baking and place on a wire rack to cool.

· As tempting as that hot bread is, try to let it rest a minimum of 15 minutes before slicing; an hour is even better. It will set up and be much easier to slice. Some very soft breads need even longer—as much as overnight—before they're "sliceable." Of course, the exceptions to the rule are the rustic French- and sourdough-type breads with their typical coarse texture. When you slice into a good French bread, it should be riddled with holes, both large and small.

ESSENTIAL GUIDELINES
FOR BREAD MACHINE BAKING

You will find some of these guidelines in your bread machine instruction booklet. The rest come from our personal experience as well as shared thoughts and suggestions from other bread machine bakers.

INGREDIENTS

· Breads turn out best when the ingredients are at room temperature, especially the liquids. The knowledgeable bakers at Red Star Yeast recommend an optimum liquid temperature of 80°F. Depending on the wattage of your microwave, a quick 30 to 60 seconds on HIGH will warm a cold cup of milk to about that temperature.

· Heavier breads such as the whole-grain loaves containing whole wheat, rye, oatmeal, etc., and breads containing a large quantity of extra ingredients such as raisins, nuts, seeds, grains, or cheese will not be as tall as simple white breads.

· Stay with the prescribed amounts of flour and liquids recommended for your machine. Trying to double a recipe could put an undue burden on your machine's motor and would definitely overflow the pan during baking.

· For best results, use only fresh ingredients.

· Any ingredients that were heated, roasted, or cooked should be cooled at room temperature before adding them to the rest of the ingredients in the bread pan.

· For whole-grain, cheese, or egg breads and loaves containing a high percentage of sugar or fat, select a Light Crust and/or Sweet Bread setting to avoid burnt crusts.

MEASURING INGREDIENTS

· It is very important to measure all ingredients carefully when using a bread machine. Sometimes as little as 1 tablespoon of liquid can make the difference between success and failure.

· To measure liquids properly, place the measuring cup on a level surface, pour in the liquid, then check the measurement at eye level.

· To measure flour properly, stir it first with a spoon to aerate it, then lightly spoon the flour into the measuring cup (do not press it in with the back of the spoon or tap the sides of the measuring cup to pack it down); level it with a straight-edged knife or spatula. Don't be a flour scooper! (We know you scoopers are out there . . . we meet you all the time. You're lovely people, but knock it off!) What happens when you dip into the bag or canister of flour with your measuring cup is that you pack in several extra tablespoons of flour each time. Two or three scoops and you have a great deal of extra flour you're not aware that you're adding. If your breads are consistently heavy, small, and dry, this is probably the reason why.

· If you can't resist packing ingredients into a measuring cup, save that urge for when you're measuring shortening and brown sugar. They should be firmly pressed down into the measuring cup.

JUDGING THE DOUGH

· If you want consistently good bread each time you use your machine, take a few moments after pressing the "Start" button to observe the dough as it mixes and kneads. Don't be afraid to open the lid to do so, if you can't see through the window. Experienced hands-on bread bakers develop a sixth sense for the proper feel of well-kneaded dough and you can too, using your eyes and ears as well as your hands.

· As soon as the dough begins to form a ball (after 5 to 10 minutes of mixing), give it a healthy pinch. You're looking for a dough that is soft and pliable. Doughs that are stiff and hard to pinch will invariably bake up into short, dense loaves. If it doesn't pass the pinch test, add more liquid 1 tablespoon at a time until it does. (Think sensuous! By the end of the kneading cycle, the dough should be warm, soft, alive, and have a lot of give to it. If you were to turn it out onto the countertop, you could easily work it with one hand.)

· You'll also need to feel and observe the outer surface of the dough, once all the flour is incorporated. It should be smooth and slightly tacky to the touch. At this point if it's either too wet and sticky or too dry and crumbly, you can make adjustments that will correct the problem. If too wet, add more flour as it kneads, 1 tablespoon at a time. If dry and crumbly, add more liquid 1 tablespoon at a time. Allow the flour or liquid to be fully absorbed by the dough each time before adding additional tablespoons. Normally, it's only a matter of 1 or 2 additional tablespoons of liquid or flour to correct the problem.

· If you have to add flour or water to the recipe, jot down what you did so that in the future you will not have to spend time observing and feeling the dough each time, unless the weather is unusually humid or dry.

· In addition to using your sense of sight and touch to judge a dough, learn to also use your sense of hearing. It is important to listen to your machine as it goes about mixing and kneading the dough. If your dough is too heavy or stiff, your machine will struggle and strain to mix it. It may even begin to stall. To alleviate the stress on your bread machine's motor, add more liquid, 1 tablespoon at a time, to soften the dough and facilitate kneading. Listen closely again. You may even detect a soft sigh from your machine and a whispered "thank you."

· The other time it's advantageous to take a quick peek at the dough is near the end of the final rising stage, shortly before it starts to bake. "Oven spring," which we describe on pages 12 and 13, also applies to the bread machine. Have you noticed how your bread takes a final jump in height during the first 8 to 10 minutes of baking? That's "oven spring." So if your dough is already nearing the lid of your machine at the end of the rising phase, you have a calamity about to take place. We've witnessed many a loaf flow down the side of the bread pan during our testings. So if you can catch it in time, a prick or two with a toothpick to deflate the top of the loaf will save you from a monumental cleanup job later on. (Flour and water baked onto the interior of your bread machine for an hour puts super glue to shame!)

The Weather Can Affect Your Breads

· We'll discuss this in length later on, but if you're a new bread baker, you need to know from the beginning that the weather can sometimes play havoc with your loaves. (It's also comforting to have something other than "pilot error" to blame those duds on, once in a while.)

· If it is exceptionally humid, dry, cold, hot—any extreme in climatic conditions—you need to make adjustments when adding your ingredients. See the Helpful Hints chapter (page 85) for specific advice.

Delayed Bake Timer

· Always keep the yeast dry when using the delayed timer setting. The moment the yeast combines with the liquids, it begins to activate. To prevent it from activating prematurely, place all liquid ingredients in the bottom of the bread pan, followed by the dry ingredients on top. Make a well in the flour for the yeast. (Panasonic bread machines have a yeast dispenser; keeping the yeast separate is no problem.)

· Do not use any items on the delayed timer setting that would spoil when left out of the refrigerator for several hours. Such items would include milk, eggs, buttermilk, sour cream, and cottage cheese. Water plus powdered substitutes can be used to replace the milk, eggs, and buttermilk in recipes listing those ingredients.

Measurements/Conversions

1½ teaspoons = ½ tablespoon
3 teaspoons = 1 tablespoon
4 tablespoons = ¼ cup
5⅓ tablespoons = ⅓ cup
16 tablespoons = 1 cup

⅛ cup = 2 tablespoons
⅜ cup = ¼ cup + 2 tablespoons
⅝ cup = ½ cup + 2 tablespoons
⅞ cup = ¾ cup + 2 tablespoons
1⅛ cup = 1 cup + 2 tablespoons

2 tablespoons = ⅛ cup = 1 ounce
8 tablespoons = ½ cup = 4 ounces
16 tablespoons = 1 cup = 8 ounces = ½ pint
2 cups = 16 ounces = 1 pint = ½ quart
4 cups = 32 ounces = 2 pints = 1 quart
8 cups = 64 ounces = 4 pints = 2 quarts = ½ gallon
16 cups = 128 ounces = 8 pints = 4 quarts = 1 gallon

1 cup all-purpose flour = 130 grams = 4.59 ounces
1 cup bread flour = 135 grams = 4.76 ounces

1 cup whole wheat flour = 128 grams = 4.51 ounces
4 ounces grated cheese = 1 cup
1 stick of butter = 8 tablespoons = ½ cup = ¼ pound
1 pound of butter = 2 cups
1 large egg = scant ¼ cup liquid
1 lemon = 2 to 3 tablespoons juice
1 lemon = 4 teaspoons grated rind
1 medium orange = 6 to 8 tablespoons juice
1 medium orange = 1 ½ tablespoons grated rind

· To measure flour properly, stir it first with a spoon to aerate it, then lightly spoon the flour into a measuring cup (do not press it in with the back of the spoon or tap the sides of the measuring cup to pack it down); level it with a straight-edged knife or spatula. Do not scoop flour out of the bag or cannister with the measuring cup. You'll end up with an extra tablespoon or two of flour per cup, enough to make a big difference in your bread.

· Measure liquids by placing the measuring cup on a level surface, pour in the liquid, then check the measurement at eye level. A clear glass or plastic liquid measuring cup is essential. Do not use your dry measuring cup.

· Shortening and brown sugar should be firmly packed into the measuring cup before leveling off.

3
Ingredients

WHEAT FLOURS

The wheat berry consists of an outer layer (the bran), a small embryo inside (the germ), and the starchy interior (the endosperm), which provides food for the developing seed. Bread flour, which is the milled endosperm of hard winter and spring wheat kernels, has the highest gluten content among the white flours, and it produces the highest rising loaves. Spring wheat flour is planted in the spring and is harvested late summer; winter wheat is planted in the fall but lies dormant under winter snows and is later harvested in the early summer. Spring wheats are generally a little higher in gluten than winter wheats.

Whole wheat flour contains all elements of the wheat kernel: the germ, the bran, and the endosperm. For that reason, it also contains more nutrients, fiber, and natural oils. Whole wheat breads are denser and usually less tall than strictly white flour loaves.

Milling grains today usually involves grinding them between rapidly rotating steel cylinders until crushed, or smashing them with swiftly moving steel hammer heads, turning the grains to powder instantly. Both methods involve speed and high temperatures. Stone-ground flour, as the name suggests, is crushed between stone mills, but at a much slower pace and lower temperature than the more modern methods. The value of the "old-fashioned" stone milling process is that nutrients are not lost to the excessive heat and oxidation created by the more "efficient" methods.

White flour should be stored in airtight containers in a cool (75°F or less), dry location. If properly stored, the shelf life for commercial flour is 15 months from the coded date on the back of the package. (To decipher the date, simply call the 800 number listed on the package for directions.)

If you have a problem with weevils during the warm summer months, place newly purchased flour in the freezer for several days. Then store it in a tightly sealed container. You shouldn't have any further problems with "unwelcome guests."

Whole wheat and any other whole-grain flours should be kept under refrigeration to prevent the natural oils in the wheat germ and bran from turning rancid. If you choose to freeze them, know that freezing destroys vitamin E. (Note: If you plan to hand-mill your own grains, grind only enough flour for immediate use. Freshly ground flour will turn rancid rapidly and begin to lose valuable nutrients within two to three days. The raw grains, however, will keep indefinitely.)

ALL-PURPOSE FLOUR

· All-purpose flour is a blend of hard and soft wheats and was created to be a single flour that would work well in all recipes from delicate cakes to hearty breads.

· All-purpose flour is the milled starchy endosperm of the wheat kernel. The bran and wheat germ have been removed. Its natural yellowish tinge has been chemically whitened, usually with a chlorine gas.

· The average protein/gluten content is 10 to 11 percent.

· Breads baked in the bread machine using all-purpose bleached or unbleached flour will be significantly smaller than those made with bread flour with its higher amount of gluten.

UNBLEACHED FLOUR

· Unbleached flour is an all-purpose flour that has whitened with age; however, that aging process may have been chemically accelerated.

BREAD FLOUR

· Bread flour produces the highest loaves. You will find it in the market labeled "bread flour" or "Better for Bread Flour."

· Bread flour is also ground from the endosperm of the wheat kernel, but it is composed of strictly hard wheat flour, not a mixture of hard and soft wheat like all-purpose flour.

· The protein/gluten content of bread flour can be anywhere from 12 to 16 percent; usually, it's right around 14 percent.

· Gluten absorbs water; consequently, a bread-flour dough requires more liquid than a dough made from all-purpose flour.

· Some bread flours have potassium bromate added. It strengthens the gluten; higher loaves are a result. This is known as "bromated flour," which some bread machine manufacturers recommend. Other commercial bread flours contain ascorbic acid (vitamin C) instead of potassium bromate. It, too, aids in creating higher-rising loaves.

Self-Rising Flour

· Baking soda and salt have been added to all-purpose flour to create self-rising flour. Self-rising flour is not recommended for use in bread machine recipes because it has less gluten than bread flour and a higher sodium content. It is best used in non-yeast baked goods.

Cake/Pastry Flour

· Again, these flours are obviously better suited for purposes other than bread baking. They are both milled from low-gluten, soft wheat.

Instant Flour

· This flour is also not appropriate for bread baking. It usually comes in a can and because of its quick-mixing properties, is best put to use thickening sauces and gravies.

Whole Wheat Flour

· Whole wheat flour contains all three components of the wheat kernel: the bran, the germ, and the endosperm.

· Whole wheat breads will not be as tall as loaves made with bread flour. If your whole wheat breads are too small, replacing a portion of the whole wheat flour with bread flour or adding gluten will help. (You can purchase vital wheat gluten at most health food stores.)

· Usually, stone-ground wheat flour is coarser than the steel-ground whole wheat flour. The coarser the flour, the harder it is for the gluten to develop fully. As a result, breads made with stone-ground flour or coarsely ground hand-milled flour do not rise as high as other whole-grain flours. You will probably want to add gluten or some other dough enhancer and/or extra yeast.

· Whole-grain flours take longer to absorb moisture; the dough should feel more moist than a white-flour dough. If it is dry and stiff to the touch, that means it has too much flour, not enough liquid, and that it will result in a small, heavy, and very dense loaf. We all know them well—the infamous "doorstops" and "hockey pucks."

WHOLE WHEAT BREAD FLOUR

· Some health food stores sell this type of whole wheat flour. It is ground from hard wheat and has a higher gluten content than regular whole wheat flour.

· You can essentially create your own whole wheat bread flour by adding up to one tablespoon gluten to each cup of whole wheat flour.

WHITE WHOLE WHEAT FLOUR

· This is a fairly new flour on the market and not widely available as of this writing (see Sources, page 215). It's good news for those not particularly fond of the full-bodied, slightly bitter flavor of whole wheat. White whole wheat flour provides the same nutrients as whole wheat flour but has the mild, sweeter taste of white all-purpose flour.

· White whole wheat flour can be used in any recipe—even gravy—calling for all-purpose flour.

· Treat this flour as you would regular whole wheat flour; it still needs the longer kneading and rising times. The finished product resembles a loaf made with 50 percent all-purpose flour and 50 percent whole wheat flour.

WHOLE WHEAT PASTRY FLOUR

· Whole wheat pastry flour is ground from soft wheat, which means it has a low gluten content. It's comparable to cake flour and not suited for bread machine baking.

GRAHAM FLOUR

· Graham flour is soft winter wheat that resembles whole wheat flour in taste but has less protein (gluten). It will not produce as tall a loaf as regular whole wheat flour.

DURUM FLOUR

· Durum wheat, from which durum flour is ground, is the hardest of the wheats. A bread made entirely from durum wheat would be inedible.

SEMOLINA FLOUR

· Semolina flour is a refined durum flour, minus the bran and wheat germ. It is highly prized as a pasta flour. Combined with liquid and oil, it forms a very stiff dough, making possible a multitude of pasta shapes.

· Semolina flour can also be used in breads.

TRITICALE FLOUR

· Triticale is a hybrid grain—a cross between rye, durum, and red winter wheat.

· It is higher in protein than either wheat or rye flours but low in gluten. For a decent-size loaf, you need to combine it with at least an equal amount of high-gluten wheat flour.

· Triticale flour has a "ryelike" sweet, nutty flavor.

KAMUT FLOUR

· An ancient grain, kamut is a relative of durum wheat.

· It is high in protein and potassium and contains a unique type of gluten that is easier for the body to utilize than regular wheat.

· Kamut flour, though high in protein, is low in gluten. It must be combined with higher-gluten wheat flour to produce an acceptable bread.

SPELT FLOUR

· Spelt is an ancient wheat once grown in Mesopotamia that can survive very hostile growing conditions.

· Some people who are allergic to wheat find they can tolerate spelt wheat. Check with your allergist first to be sure.

· Spelt flour contains enough gluten to be an adequate substitute for wheat flours.

NON-WHEAT FLOURS

Non-wheat flours contain very small amounts of gluten; consequently, they must be combined with wheat flours to produce a normal-size loaf. We found that using a 2½:1 ratio (2½ parts wheat flour to 1 part non-wheat flour) generally worked well.

Well-stocked grocery stores now carry the most common non-wheat flours such as rye and barley, but the best place to find all these flours under one roof is a health food store. If you're interested in experimenting with one or two of the more exotic flours and your health food store doesn't carry them, refer to the list of Sources (page 215).

LIGHT/MEDIUM RYE FLOUR

· This is a light grayish-tan flour ground from the endosperm of the rye grain. It does not contain the bran or germ.

· It produces breads with a hearty, old-world country flavor.

· Rye flour is high in protein but low in gluten. You need to use at least 2 cups wheat flour for each cup rye flour to produce an acceptable loaf in a bread machine.

DARK/PUMPERNICKEL RYE FLOUR

· Ground from the whole rye grain, it contains the bran and the germ as well as the endosperm.

· It has a coarser texture than light/medium rye flour and bakes up into a darker loaf.

· This flour is usually more difficult to locate. It's best suited for the dark pumpernickels and rustic black breads.

OAT FLOUR

· If you cannot locate oat flour in your health food store, try making your own. Place rolled oats in a blender or food processor and process until finely ground. You can also create oat flour by grinding whole oat groats in a hand mill.

· Oat flour contains an antioxidant, which acts as a preservative, helping the bread to retain its freshness longer.

· It is very high in protein, low in gluten, and must be combined with wheat flour to produce an acceptable loaf.

BARLEY FLOUR

· Barley flour has a mild sweet flavor and low gluten content, and is pale gray in color.

· Barley breads should contain at least 3 cups wheat flour for every 1 cup barley flour.

· It is perishable and should be stored in the refrigerator or freezer.

· Barley flour lends a soft, almost cakelike texture to breads and a subtle sweetness to the taste.

BUCKWHEAT FLOUR

· Made from grinding buckwheat groats, this flour is high in protein, relatively high in fat, and very low in gluten.

· It's a pungent, tart, earthy-tasting flour that lends a grayish color to the finished bread. It is best used in small amounts, no more than ½ cup per loaf.

MILLET FLOUR

· Millet flour is high in protein but very low in gluten.

· It is a light, yellowish flour with a slightly gritty texture.

· Breads baked with millet flour tend to be dry and crumbly in texture. We preferred using millet flour on a 3:1 ratio (3 parts wheat flour, 1 part millet flour).

AMARANTH FLOUR

· Amaranth is higher in protein, lysine, iron, and calcium than most other grains.

· Use this low-gluten flour in combination with high-gluten wheat flour; ½ cup amaranth flour per loaf will suffice.

TEFF FLOUR

· Teff flour has been favored by the highland Ethiopians for centuries.

· This light flour has a high ratio of bran and germ because the teff grain is the smallest of all grains.

· Combine teff flour with wheat flour for an acceptable-size loaf.

STORAGE

· Whole-grain flours that still contain some or all of the bran and germ should be stored in the refrigerator or freezer. These include dark rye, barley, buckwheat, millet, amaranth, and quinoa.

GLUTEN-FREE FLOURS AND GRAINS

Brown and/or white rice flours form the basis of most gluten-free breads. To vary the flavor, substitute other gluten-free flours and grains in ¼-, ½-, or 1-cup quantities. The possible combinations are limited only by your imagination! For instance, we replaced 1 cup rice flour with 1 cup corn flour and produced a mild-flavored, great change-of-pace bread.

RICE FLOUR

· Both brown and white rice flours are available. Brown rice flour includes the rice bran and, therefore, is more nutritious and has more fat than white rice flour.

· Bread made with rice flour instead of wheat flour has a sweet flavor and chewy texture.

· Rice flour is the most common substitute for wheat flour when baking gluten-free breads.

SWEET RICE FLOUR

· This is a waxy form of rice flour that is not normally used in baked goods. It's better suited for thickening sauces.

POTATO STARCH FLOUR

· This is the finely milled starch from the potato. It helps retain the bread's moisture and freshness and aids in the fermentation of the yeast.

POTATO FLOUR

· Unlike potato starch flour, this heavy flour is made from cooked potatoes that have been dried and then ground into flour. It gives a definite potato taste to breads.

· To avoid lumping, blend it with the sugar and fat before adding liquids.

Soy Flour

· Soy flour is high in protein (amino acids), iron, and calcium.

· It has a rather bitter, beanlike flavor that some find objectionable. It should be used sparingly; start with 2 tablespoons per loaf and increase the amount in future loaves as your taste buds dictate.

· Breads made with soy flour will be moist and finely textured.

· There are both regular and low-fat soy bean flours. If using the regular flour, make sure it is fresh. Store it in the refrigerator or freezer to prevent it from going rancid.

Tapioca Flour

· Tapioca flour is processed from the roots of the cassava plant.

Corn Flour

· A low-protein flour with a sweet flavor.

· Yellow or white corn can be milled into a fine flour.

Quinoa Flour

· Quinoa flour is very high in protein and has a nutty taste.

· This ancient flour is very similar to amaranth flour in nutrition and history.

· It can also be used to make gluten-free pasta.

Legume Flours

· These gluten-free flours include pea, mung, lentil, soy, and garbanzo bean flours.

· Created by grinding various beans, they add their own unique personality to breads.

Cornmeal

· Cornmeal is coarsely ground yellow, white, or blue corn.

· Add ½ cup cornmeal to gluten-free breads and it will give the loaf a crumbly texture and sweet taste.

· Store freshly milled cornmeal in the refrigerator for 2 to 3 weeks at the most.

QUINOA

· This tiny grain should be rinsed well before using to remove any traces of its bitter coating.

· Add up to ½ cup whole quinoa to gluten-free breads for a sweet, nutty taste.

STORAGE

· Store corn flour, brown rice flour, soy flour, and cornmeal in the refrigerator or freezer to prevent rancidity.

WHOLE GRAINS

These are all the wonderful "extras" that add so much flavor, texture, and wholesome goodness to whole-grain breads. They can be cooked, toasted, soaked, or sprouted and then added to your bread. Some, like rolled oats and cornmeal, can be used as is. (If rolled grains, meals, flakes, or cereals are added to the mix dry, they will soak up moisture from the dough, causing it to be a dry or crumbly bread. Be sure to add extra liquid when adding dry, uncooked grains to your dough.)

You can add as little as 1 tablespoon whole grains per cup of flour or as much as ¼ cup whole grains per cup of flour to your breads; your taste buds and the bread's density and texture should be your guide. The more grains you add, the heavier, denser, and more crumbly the bread will be. It will also be more nutritious. Whole grains can simply be added to your favorite bread; no need to delete a like amount of flour. Watch the dough as it kneads and add more liquid or flour if necessary.

As a general rule of thumb, whole grains such as wheat berries, kamut, whole oats, and triticale should be soaked in water overnight, then simmered on the stovetop in a covered saucepan for 30 to 60 minutes, until they are tender. Drain them well in a colander. Rice, barley, rye, amaranth, quinoa, buckwheat groats (kasha), millet, teff, and cracked wheat do not require soaking to soften them before being cooked. Remember to let the grains cool before adding them to your bread dough in quantities up to ¼ cup whole grain per cup of flour.

To sprout whole grains: rinse them first, then cover them with warm water and let stand at room temperature for approximately 15 hours. Drain off the water and rinse the berries in fresh water. Place them in a clean glass jar, cover the top with a damp piece of cheese cloth, and secure it with a rubber band. Set the jar on its side and place it in a warm, dark spot. Rinse the berries with fresh water every 12 hours until they begin to sprout (no need to remove the cheesecloth each time). At this point they are ready to be used in a recipe. The whole process should take 2 to 3 days. Use approximately ¼ cup sprouted berries per cup of flour. Be sure to drain them well first.

You can toast grains such as oats, millet, amaranth, and quinoa in a skillet over medium heat or in a baking pan, in a 300°F oven for 10 to 15 minutes. Watch closely to avoid scorching them.

Whole Wheat Berries

· You should be able to find red winter or spring wheat kernels in your local health food store. They're teeth crunchers if you attempt to eat them raw, but if you sprout them first, they'll be much more edible (and less hazardous). Sprouted wheat will add a surprising sweet taste and moistness to your breads.

· They can also be cooked and added to the bread dough. To cook, soak whole wheat berries overnight in water, then drain them and add 1 cup of the soaked kernels to 3½ cups boiling water. Bring the water back to a boil, cover the saucepan with a lid, reduce the heat to low, and simmer for 50 to 60 minutes until tender.

· Well-drained cooked or sprouted wheat berries can be added to your breads in quantities up to ¼ cup berries per cup of flour.

· If you are interested in milling your own flours, we've found that 1 cup whole wheat kernels produces approximately 1¾ cups medium-ground whole wheat flour.

WHEAT BRAN

· The bran is the outer hull of the wheat kernel. It does contain some fat.

· Wheat bran is usually sold as "miller's bran" or "unprocessed bran flakes" in grocery and health food stores.

· Bran adds fiber, texture, and flavor to homemade breads.

· Limit the amount of wheat bran used in recipes to ¼ cup per cup of flour. The sharp edges of the bran cut the gluten strands and thereby reduce the bread's elasticity.

· You can either add bran to a favorite recipe (plus some additional liquid) or replace part of the flour with bran (which will produce a heavier, smaller loaf).

· Store bran in a cool, dry place up to 1 month, 3 months in the refrigerator, or up to 1 year in the freezer.

WHEAT GERM

· The germ is the embryo of the wheat kernel. Added to breads, it increases its nutritional value and adds a nutty flavor.

· In large quantities, wheat germ will inhibit the gluten's growth. Use no more than 2 tablespoons in the larger 1½-pound loaves or 1½ tablespoons in 1-pound loaves. It isn't necessary to reduce the amount of flour when adding wheat germ to a recipe.

· Wheat germ contains a great deal of natural oil. To prevent rancidity, store it in the refrigerator or in the freezer; however, freezing will destroy the germ's vitamin E.

CRACKED WHEAT

· These are whole wheat berries that have been broken into rather large pieces. Again, they are too hard to eat as is; they need to be softened first by cooking them. To cook, add 1 cup cracked wheat to 2⅓ cups boiling water, return water to a boil, stir, cover, and simmer on low heat for 15 minutes.

· As a rule, add no more than ¼ cup well-drained, cooked cracked wheat per cup of flour to a favorite bread.

BULGUR

· Bulgur is cracked wheat that has also been parboiled; consequently, it will absorb liquids faster than cracked wheat. Uncooked and added to bread doughs it will give a flavorful, crunchy texture to your breads.

· To soften it, soak 1 cup bulgur in 2 cups boiling water for ½ hour, then drain and cool.

· As with cooked cracked wheat, drain bulgur well and add a maximum of ¼ cup bulgur per cup of flour to any recipe for additional fiber and nutrients.

WHOLE WHEAT FLAKES

· These flakes of wheat resemble rolled oats. They're created by heating and pressing whole wheat berries.

· You may have passed them by without ever noticing them. Check the bulk bins or the packaged grains more closely next time you visit your local health food store.

· Experiment by substituting whole wheat flakes for wheat bran or oatmeal in a recipe.

WHOLE RYE BERRIES

· As the wheat berry is to whole wheat flour, the rye berry is to dark rye flour. These kernels can be sprouted and then added to any of your rye breads for extra flavor in quantities up to ¼ cup sprouted berries per cup of flour. They are an additional ingredient, not a substitution for flour.

· Rye berries can also be ground into a dark rye flour.

· To cook whole rye berries, place 1 cup of the grain into 3 cups boiling water. Return the water to a boil, cover, reduce the heat, and simmer for 1 hour.

CRACKED WHOLE RYE

· On the off chance that you might be able to locate this grain, treat it much the same as cracked wheat. It needs to be cooked before it is added to bread doughs. To 3½ cups boiling water, add 1 cup cracked whole rye. Return to a boil, cover the pot, and allow to simmer for 30 minutes.

· Cooked and well-drained, cracked whole rye can be added to your favorite rye breads in ¼-cup-per-cup-of-flour quantities. A like amount of flour does not need to be omitted from the recipe.

Whole Rye Flakes

· If you were lucky enough to find cracked whole rye, set your sights for whole rye flakes next. Just like wheat and rolled oat flakes, they're whole rye berries that have been heated and pressed flat.

· Substitute rye flakes in recipes calling for rolled oats for a change of flavor.

Rolled Oats

· The inedible husk that surrounds the oat kernel is removed; the grain is then sliced, steamed, rolled, and dried to produce rolled oats.

· Quick-cooking oats are rolled flatter and heat treated longer than regular oats, making them faster cooking.

· We recommend old-fashioned rolled oats, not the quick-cooking variety in bread recipes. We think they hold up better.

· Oats add a sweet, nutty, taste and chewy texture to bread. To intensify that flavor, you can toast them first.

· Breads containing oats stay fresher longer due to the natural antioxidant found in the oat's endosperm.

· For a change of pace, try adding up to 1 cup cooked oatmeal to your bread dough. You can use it as a replacement for the oats in an oatmeal bread or as an additional ingredient in a bread of your choice. (Don't forget to decrease the liquid in your recipe to allow for the moisture in the oatmeal.)

Oat Groats

· Akin to wheat berries and whole rye berries, oat groats are the raw oat kernels with the outer hull removed. Like wheat and rye berries, they need to be soaked overnight and then cooked to make them edible.

· To cook, place 1 cup of oat groats (that have soaked overnight) in 3 cups boiling water, return to a boil, cover the pan, reduce the heat to low, and simmer the groats for 30 minutes.

· Like wheat berries, add up to ¼ cup cooked and drained oat groats per cup of flour in any recipe you choose. You won't need to reduce the flour by the equivalent amount; however, you may need to adjust the liquid/flour balance in your dough while it kneads.

STEEL-CUT OATS

· As their name suggests, these oat kernels have been thinly sliced with sharp steel blades, then heat-processed.

· This firm-textured cooked cereal is also known as Scottish oatmeal.

· Cook steel-cut oats, uncovered, in boiling water as you would rolled oats until they begin to thicken (15 minutes); cool, then add to breads in quantities up to 1 cup per loaf.

· You can use cooked oats as a replacement for rolled in an oatmeal bread (reduce the liquid in your recipe accordingly) or as an additional ingredient in other breads.

OAT BRAN

· Because of its blood cholesterol–lowering properties, oat bran is a very popular addition to homemade bread.

· Oat bran contains twice the soluble fiber of rolled oats.

· Use oat bran sparingly in bread doughs—¼ cup oat bran per cup of flour. Just as wheat bran does, oat bran detracts from the gluten's structure and elasticity.

· You can add bran to a favorite recipe (plus some additional liquid) or replace part of the flour with bran (which will produce a heavier, smaller loaf).

BARLEY

· Pearled barley has had the outer hull removed and much of the bran and germ.

· Whole, hull-less barley contains the bran and germ; only the inedible outer hull has been removed.

· To cook barley, rinse it well, add 1 cup grain to 3½ cups boiling water, return the water to a boil, then cover, reduce the heat to low, and simmer for 30 to 35 minutes.

· Use hull-less barley rather than pearled barley for sprouting.

· When you include sprouted barley in your bread, it adds a wonderful, sweet flavor. Add as much as ¼ cup well-drained sprouted barley per cup of flour.

· Sprouted barley can also be dried and ground to create diastatic malt powder, which is a natural dough enhancer and sugar substitute. It converts the flour's starch into sugar.

CORNMEAL

· Cornmeal is coarsely ground yellow, white, or blue corn.

· Added to bread, it will give it a crumbly texture and a sweet taste. It also weakens the gluten's strength, so ⅓ cup in a 3-cup flour recipe is the maximum.

· Cornmeal that is "degerminated" has had the germ removed. Water-ground or stone-ground cornmeal still contains the germ.

· Cornmeal is very sweet tasting when freshly ground. If it has a strong, bitter smell and taste, it is stale.

· Store freshly milled cornmeal in the refrigerator for 2 to 3 weeks at most.

BUCKWHEAT GROATS (KASHA)

· Buckwheat is not a grain; it's actually a member of the rhubarb family.

· Add as much as ¼ cup of this pungent kernel to your breads in its cooked form (kasha) for each cup of flour in the recipe. It should be used as an additional ingredient rather than a flour substitute. You may need to reduce the liquid in the recipe or add an extra tablespoon or more of flour while the dough is kneading if it appears too wet.

MILLET

· Millet is a tiny, yellow, round grain with a mild flavor. It's high in protein and easily digested.

· You can add it as is to bread to give your loaves an interesting new texture and some extra crunch in each bite.

TRITICALE

· This whole grain is a cross between hard red wheat, durum wheat, and rye. It's the very first man-made grain.

· It can be sprouted, cooked, or ground into flour just like other whole grains.

· To cook triticale, first soak 1 cup berries in water overnight. Next day, add the drained berries to 3 cups boiling water, return the water to a boil, cover, reduce the heat to low, and simmer for 60 to 70 minutes.

· Add well-drained sprouted or cooked triticale berries to your breads for extra nutrition in quantities of up to ¼ cup berries per cup of flour.

AMARANTH

· This ancient grain's history dates back to the Aztecs in Mexico and Central America.

· Amaranth is not a grass like most other grains; it's a leaf plant belonging to the spinach family.

· This tiny, high-protein grain looks like cream-colored poppy seeds. It will add a sweet, nutty flavor to your breads.

· This extra ingredient for your breads can be added in quantities up to ¼ cup grain per cup of flour. It is not a flour substitute.

QUINOA

· Similar to amaranth, this ancient grain was a staple in years past for the Inca civilization.

· It is also nutritionally very similar to amaranth.

· Rinse this grain well before using to remove any traces of its bitter coating. (Dry it well, too, if you plan to grind it into flour.)

· Add as much as ¼ cup quinoa per cup of flour to your breads. You do not need to decrease the flour in the recipe by an equal amount.

KAMUT

· The kamut kernel has a buttery taste and is three times larger than a grain of wheat.

· It is a relative of durum wheat and should be cooked and cooled before adding it to your breads. To cook kamut, first soak 1 cup of the kernels in water overnight. The following day, add the drained kamut to 3 cups boiling water. Bring the water back to a boil, cover, reduce the heat, and simmer the grain for 30 to 40 minutes until tender.

· Once cooled and well drained, add at most only ¼ cup kamut for every cup of flour in the recipe. It should be used as an additional ingredient, not a flour substitute.

SORGHUM

· This milletlike grain can be used whole or ground into a sweet meal or flour for your breads.

YEAST

Yeast is a living organism, a single-cell plant. One pound of active dry yeast contains more than 3 billion of those yeast cells! There are about 160 known species of yeast but the one we're concerned with is the *saccharomyces cerevisiae* species. Different strains of it are used for active dry, compressed, fast-rising, and instant yeast. It's the same species of yeast used in brewing beer and wine; that's why it was also called "brewer's yeast" (not to be confused with the nutritional yeast of the same name that has no leavening properties because the yeast cells are dead). Active yeast organisms are found in high concentrations in the foam of newly made beer and wine. Initially, before the convenient little packets of active dry yeast came into being, bread bakers had to obtain their yeast from the local brewery. Imagine having to visit the local brewery/winery to bring home a cup of foam every time you felt like baking bread in your machine!

Since we now live in a more modern world, instead of begging a cup of foam from your local brewmeister, we recommend that you buy your yeast in 1-pound or 2-pound bulk packages at warehouse discount clubs, restaurant supply stores, or from bulk bins in health food stores. Initially, you'll look at that huge package of yeast and feel certain that you could never use it up in your lifetime. Trust us . . . you will! If you're still timid about buying that much yeast, or don't have easy access to a supplier, most markets now carry the convenient 4-ounce glass jars of active dry yeast.

As you'll notice in our recipes, we're partial to Red Star yeast. We stumbled on their product quite by accident and, because of what we found to be superior results, we've used and recommended it ever since. It is easily obtainable and reasonably priced, especially when bought in bulk. We've turned to the experts at Red Star many times for sound bread-baking advice. They're extremely busy people and we don't want to encourage anyone just to call and chitchat, but if you ever have yeast-related questions, you'll find everyone there very pleasant and helpful. Red Star's number is listed in the back of this book in the Sources section under Universal Foods Corporation (page 217).

THE FERMENTATION PROCESS

· Yeast is activated when it comes in contact with a warm liquid. To grow, it needs food (sugars), warmth, a slightly acidic environment, and some oxygen.

· The fermentation process begins with the yeast's consumption of available sugars. The first sugars it takes in are glucose, fructose, and the combination of the two: sucrose (table sugar). When those initial sugar supplies are depleted, it then feeds on maltose, the sugar created when the malt enzymes present in the dough convert some of the flour's starch into sugar.

· If you have the "If-some-is-good, more-is-better" outlook on life, it won't play well when adding sugar to bread dough. True, some added sugar will help stimulate the yeast's growth, but large quantities will actually have the opposite effect.

· As the yeast feeds, it multiplies, and gives off two by-products: carbon dioxide and alcohol. Though the alcohol gives bread its wonderful aroma and flavor, if the dough is left too long to ferment (rise), the alcohol will eventually kill the yeast and produce a very bitter-tasting bread. Punching the dough down releases carbon dioxide gasses and allows some of the accumulated alcohol to evaporate.

· Yeast dough rises best at temperatures between 80° and 85°F.

· Salt is a necessary inhibitor of yeast's growth and also helps to strengthen the gluten's structure. If you omit the salt in recipes, it's most likely that your loaves will "overproof"—rise up very high then collapse when the heat is turned on.

· Salt, in high concentration, can also kill the yeast if the two come in contact as you're adding ingredients to the bread pan. Take care to keep them separated.

· Yeast doesn't respond well when it's doused with oil prior to mixing. So be good to your yeast. Add the oil to the liquids in the bottom of the pan, then the dry ingredients, and the yeast last.

ACTIVE DRY YEAST

· One ¼-ounce packet of yeast equals 2¼ teaspoons yeast.

· Active dry yeast is available in strips of three ¼-ounce packets, 4-ounce jars, and 2-pound bulk packages.

· When using active dry yeast in a recipe made without a bread machine, the ideal liquid temperature is between 105° and 115°F. Testing at Red Star, however, has shown that a lower liquid temperature of 80°F yields the best results when baking breads in a bread machine. If you don't have a thermometer, 80°F water is in the "warm" range—not "cold," not "hot," but basically room temperature.

FAST-ACTING YEASTS

· Rapid-Rise, Quick-Rise, and Instant are all fast-acting yeasts. They cut the bread's rising time almost in half, but are also the James Deans of the yeast family; they live fast, give a stellar performance, but die young. For this reason, fast-acting yeasts are not well suited for multiple risings, long periods of fermentation (French breads, sourdoughs), or the long whole-wheat cycle on some bread machines.

· Fast-acting yeasts are available in strips of three ¼-ounce packets, 4-ounce jars, and 1-pound bulk packages.

· Fast-acting yeasts can be used in both the bread machine's Regular and Rapid Bake cycles. Use ½ teaspoon fast-acting yeast per cup of flour in the Regular cycle. When testing the fast-acting yeasts in the Rapid Bake cycle, we had much better results when we doubled the amount of yeast (1 teaspoon per cup of flour). We did find, however, that fast-acting yeast did not work as well as regular active dry yeast on either cycle in some machines.

· If your bread rises up beautifully but collapses once baking begins, try reducing the amount of fast-acting yeast in that particular recipe next time. (For other remedies, see our suggestions in the Helpful Hints section beginning on page 89.)

· Instant active dry yeast is very similar to rapid/quick-rise yeasts and can be used interchangeably with it. Use ½ teaspoon instant yeast per cup of flour in the Regular cycle; double that amount for the Rapid Bake cycle.

BREAD MACHINE YEAST

· The popularity of the bread machine has inspired this specially formulated yeast. In addition to yeast, it contains ascorbic acid and an emulsifier which produces loaves that are taller and lighter than those baked with regular active dry or instant yeast.

· It is available in 7-ounce jars.

COMPRESSED (FRESH) YEAST

· Compressed yeast is sold in ⅗-ounce cakes and can usually be found in the deli cases of most markets. It must be kept refrigerated (up to 2 weeks) or frozen (up to 2 months). Once thawed, fresh yeast should be used right away.

· One ⅗-ounce cake of compressed yeast equals one ¼-ounce packet of active dry yeast.

· When fresh, it is light tan in color. If it has gone past its prime, it will turn brown.

· Compressed yeast should be dissolved in liquids no warmer than 95°F. Temperatures approaching 120°F will kill it.

· Most professional bakers use compressed yeast rather than active dry yeast. They prefer its lower activating temperature and find it more dependable to work with. Its very limited shelf life is no problem for them.

· Compressed yeast is not recommended by any bread machine manufacturers, but in our tests we found that it produced nicely shaped loaves that were, on average, one inch smaller than those made with active dry yeast. The disadvantage to the cake yeast is that its shelf life is approximately two weeks (or two months if frozen), making it very inconvenient. It's also more expensive to use.

HOW TO DETERMINE IF YOUR YEAST IS STILL ACTIVE

· In a 1-cup glass measuring cup, dissolve 1 teaspoon sugar in ½ cup warm water (110° to 115°F). Sprinkle 1 scant tablespoon yeast slowly over the surface. Stir; allow the mixture to sit for 10 minutes. Within the first 5 minutes, the yeast should begin rising to the surface. At the end of 10 minutes' time, if the yeast has doubled and reached the 1 cup mark and has a rounded crown of foam, it is very active. Yeast that is inactive or losing its potency will either not react at all or will not reach the 1-

cup mark within 10 minutes. In either case, discard that package of yeast and buy a new one.

· If your breads suddenly bake up very small and dense, try testing your yeast before continuing.

· If you buy your yeast in bulk bins at health food stores, we recommend you test it before using it.

STORAGE

· Yeast deteriorates when it is exposed to heat, moisture, and oxygen.

· Active-dry and fast-acting yeasts should be kept in a cool, dry location. You can store the 3-strip packets at room temperature (use before the expiration date stamped on the package) or you can store the packets and the 4-ounce jars of yeast in the refrigerator.

· If you purchase the yeast in 1- or 2-pound bulk packages, remove a small quantity and store it in an airtight glass jar in the refrigerator. The remainder of the yeast should be well-wrapped, placed in a plastic bag, and stored in the freezer. Replenish your small jar of yeast with the frozen yeast as needed. Though the bulk package is not stamped with an expiration date, if you store it in the freezer, you will find that you'll use it up long before the yeast loses it potency. The bulk package will keep in the freezer at least one year. (By the way, Red Star bulk yeast is vacuum packed. We've known people who were hesitant to purchase it because it felt like a solid brick of yeast. They thought they'd have difficulty breaking off chunks and measuring it. Actually, when you open the package, that "brick of yeast" turns granular instantly. It never ceases to amaze and delight us. Sometimes it's even the high point of our day!)

· **One caution:** If you store your yeast in the refrigerator or freezer, do not zap it in the microwave to bring it to room temperature quickly. Like any living organism, yeast doesn't take kindly to microwaving.

LIQUIDS

The liquids bind all the ingredients together in a bread dough as well as activate the yeast's performance. There is a large selection of liquids to bake with and each will affect your bread in different ways.

WATER

· Breads using water as the only liquid have a crisper crust.

· The acidity or alkalinity of your tap water can have a dramatic effect on your breads. Very soft (acidic) water results in soft and sticky bread doughs due to poorly developed gluten. On the other hand, very hard (alkaline) water retards the yeast's fermentation. The happy medium for your bread dough is tap water with a slightly acidic pH balance.

· If you wish to determine the pH balance of your water, call your local water authority or health department. A pH of 7 is neutral. A pH from 5.5 to 6.5 would be perfect. (To give you the broader picture: orange juice has an acidic pH of 3.0, distilled water has an acidic pH of 5.5, milk has a 6.9 pH. On the other side of the scale, baking soda mixed in water has an alkaline 8.4 pH.)

· Once you determine your water's pH balance, you can counteract very hard water by adding about 1 to 1 ½ teaspoons lemon juice or vinegar to the tap water in your recipe. If you have very soft water, adding ¼ teaspoon baking soda to your recipe or replacing 2 tablespoons of your water with an egg white should return your bread dough to its most yeast-friendly state. In either case, a third option is to use a good-quality bottled water.

· Do not use softened water; it has a very high sodium content.

· The very best water to use is bottled spring water. It has no chlorine and contains all the minerals the yeast needs to do its job well.

MILK

· Using milk as the liquid results in a bread with a golden brown color and a softer crust than those baked with water. It also adds a softer, finer texture and gives each slice its creamy white color.

· All milks can be used interchangeably with each other in bread recipes. By replacing whole milk with skim, all you "sacrifice" is fat.

· Certified raw milk contains certain enzymes that will interfere with the yeast's action. Scalding it first will destroy those enzymes.

NONFAT DRY MILK

· You can replace fresh milk in any recipe with water and several tablespoons nonfat dry milk powder. We generally use about 3 tablespoons powdered milk per cup of water. (Add the milk powder with the rest of the dry ingredients and keep it from mixing with the water if you plan to use the delayed-bake timer.)

· Store unopened powdered milk in a cool, dry place and don't keep it longer than a year. If your kitchen is quite warm, use it within a few months. It will eventually go bad and develop a strong, undesirable taste.

· Once opened, it is best to store nonfat dry milk in a tightly sealed container in the refrigerator, where it will remain fresh for a few months. It can also be stored at room temperature but doesn't fare well in humid weather.

· Lois buys her nonfat dry milk in bulk at a health food store. Linda buys the box of powdered milk that contains 10 quart-size, sealed envelopes at the grocery store.

BUTTERMILK

Most buttermilk is made with lowfat or skim milk that is first heated then cooled to room temperature. Next are added cultured bacteria that convert some of the milk sugar (lactose) into lactic acid. This gives buttermilk its distinctive thickness and tangy taste.

· It's the lactic acid that gives buttermilk breads a very tender crumb. Lactic acid also discourages bacterial growth, making it possible to keep buttermilk on hand longer than regular milk.

· You can create an acceptable substitute by adding 1 tablespoon distilled white vinegar or lemon juice to warm skim or low-fat milk. Stir and allow it to stand for 5 minutes.

· Buttermilk seems to vary considerably from brand to brand in flavor, acidity, and consistency. Once you find a brand you like, make a note of it.

· You just opened a quart of buttermilk to use 1⅛ cups in a buttermilk bread recipe. Now what? Well, if there are no buttermilk guzzlers in your family, our suggestion is to measure out 1⅛-cup quantities into separate, small containers and pop them into the freezer. Then you'll have buttermilk on hand when you decide to bake that bread again.

· Buttermilk will separate when frozen, so when you need it, thaw, and then shake vigorously before using.

POWDERED BUTTERMILK

· Powdered buttermilk is the perfect solution for those of you who don't have room in your freezer for cartons of buttermilk and use it only occasionally in breads.

· Use it just as you would nonfat dry milk powder; add 3 to 4 tablespoons powder per cup of water to the dry ingredients.

· Some very clever bread bakers on the Prodigy network noticed a significant difference in a particular bread baked with fresh buttermilk and the same bread baked with buttermilk powder. Several tests done with litmus strips proved their initial hunch to be correct: fresh buttermilk has a higher acid content than powdered. The recipe called for baking soda. That was okay in combination with the more acidic fresh buttermilk but it neutralized any beneficial effects the less-acidic powdered buttermilk might have had. The bottom line is, if you chose to use powdered buttermilk and the recipe also calls for baking soda, omit the baking soda.

OTHER LIQUIDS

· You can recapture some of those "lost" nutrients from the water in which you cooked vegetables or beans by using it as all, or part of, the liquid in your next bread. (If you plan to do this, avoid salting your vegetables or beans until you have removed them from the cooking water.)

· The water in which you boiled potatoes is another useful liquid. You will receive several added benefits: extra nutrients, a boost for the yeast, richer flavor, softer texture, and breads that stay fresh longer. So, save that water!

· Speaking of vegetables, many of them contain a high degree of water (the same goes for fruits). If you toss in "a little of this and a little of that" (leftover veggies from dinner or the fruit your children bypassed at breakfast), the bread you're about to make may surprise you when it turns into one big gooey puddle in the bottom of your bread pan. When adding extra fruits or vegetables, the best place to start is by calculating half their measure to be water. In other words, if you were to add 1 cup chopped apples or 1 cup chopped onion to a bread recipe, assume that you're adding ½ cup water, also. Reduce the liquid in the recipe by ½ cup. Observe the dough as it mixes. If it appears too dry, you can add liquid 1 tablespoon at a time to correct it.

· Beer can be used as a liquid; it seems to match up best with whole wheat or whole-grain breads. For the most flavor, use dark heavy beers. It helps to pour some in a cup, leave it out overnight, and let it go flat before trying to measure it.

FATS

· Fats—butter, margarine, shortening, oil—add tenderness and flavor to breads, and keep the loaves from turning stale rapidly. (By coating the starch granules, fats slow down the moisture loss that causes staling.)

· Fats also contribute to the gluten's elasticity, making for higher rising loaves. As with sugar, however, too much added fat will have just the opposite effect on the gluten and result in a very heavy, compact loaf.

· You may use just about any of the fats interchangeably, but highly flavorful oils such as olive oil, sesame oil, etc., may throw off the flavor of sweet, delicate breads.

· If you use butter, unsalted sweet butter is normally fresher than salted butter; Salt is a preservative, so salted butter is often older. Unsalted butter spoils faster; store it in the freezer.

· If the recipe calls for more than 2 tablespoons butter, cut it into several chunks, to facilitate mixing.

· We discuss fat substitutes in the next section. For those watching their fat intake (and who isn't these days), you'll be happy to know that most breads can be successfully baked with little or no fat.

SALT

· Some salt is necessary when baking bread. Salt serves as a yeast inhibitor. It "chaperones" the multiplying yeast cells, keeping their activity in check and preventing "overproofing."

· Salt prevents excess acidity in the dough, contributes to a browner crust, and prevents the growth of unwanted bacteria. It also inhibits the activity of the protein-destroying enzymes in the flour that weaken the gluten's structure.

· Without salt, one of two things would happen: Your bread would rise up very tall and then collapse during baking, or your bread would never have the proper gluten strength to rise at all. Omitting the salt from a recipe is therefore not recommended. You can, however, usually reduce the amount of salt in the recipes with no problem.

· You can also use certain salt substitutes, which we discuss in the next chapter.

· Salt enhances the flavor of all the ingredients in your bread. Without it, your oddly shaped bread would also be very flat tasting.

· Regular table salt, sea salt, and coarse kosher salt all work well in bread machine recipes.

· If you use coarse salt, increase the recipe amount by approximately 1 teaspoon to allow for its coarser texture. Add it directly to the liquids to help it dissolve completely.

· DO NOT use rock salt as a substitute for coarse kosher salt. It is not meant for human consumption.

· When adding ingredients to the bread pan, keep the salt and the yeast separated. Concentrated amounts of salt are harmful to yeast.

SWEETENERS

Sugar's role in the bread-baking process is to provide food for the ravenous yeast cells. Most or all of that food can be obtained from the flour. Powerful malt enzymes break down starch granules and convert them into maltose (malt sugar). Adding extra sugar, in moderate amounts, will increase the yeast's fermentation activity by providing additional, readily accessible food for the yeast. But a heavy hand with the sugar spoon will have a negative effect on both the yeast and the gluten. Sugar attracts water and when too much is used, it robs the yeast and gluten of needed moisture.

Sugar makes breads more moist and tender, gives the crust a lovely golden color, and, because of its moisture-attracting properties, also helps delay the staling process, which dries out bread.

There is a huge variety of sugars and each of them can add a different personality to your breads. You can often replace one sugar for another to vary the bread's flavor, but not always measure for measure. We have calculated some of those variations for you. If you substitute a "wet" sugar for a "dry" one, you should reduce your liquids by an equal measure. Observe the dough as it mixes. If it needs that missing moisture, you can always add it back in during the kneading cycle.

Handy hint of the day: When measuring sticky sugars such as honey, molasses, barley malt syrup, etc., coat your measuring spoon with a small amount of oil first. This will make the sweetener slide easily out of the spoon.

The following is a list of the sugars we were able to locate in grocery and health food stores (we have separated the "dry" granular sugars from the "wet" syrups):

GRANULATED WHITE SUGAR

· Table sugar is almost pure sucrose and has little nutritional value.

· Adding sugar to bread will help preserve its freshness, give color to the crust, and make each slice moist and tender.

· Do not substitute powdered sugar for granulated white sugar in bread recipes. Powdered sugar contains cornstarch.

BROWN SUGAR

· Brown sugar is essentially granulated white sugar crystals with a thin coating of molasses.

· The difference between light and dark brown sugars is the amount of molasses added.

· 1 tablespoon white = 1 packed tablespoon brown sugar.

· Brown sugar will slightly increase the acidic environment in your doughs.

FRUCTOSE

· Fructose, in its natural state, is the sugar found in fruits, vegetables, and honey. Commercial fructose, however, is usually obtained by breaking down sucrose into its basic elements—glucose and fructose—then separating out the fructose. Fructose created this way is a highly refined sugar, even more so than granulated white sugar.

· Fructose is almost 75 percent sweeter than granulated white sugar, giving you more sweetening power for fewer calories. To replace the sugar in recipes with fructose: 1 tablespoon sugar = a heaping 1½ teaspoons fructose.

TURBINADO SUGAR

· Turbinado sugar is partially refined sugar similar to brown sugar.

· 1 tablespoon granulated white sugar = 1 tablespoon turbinado sugar.

DATE SUGAR

· Surprisingly, since dates have the highest sugar content of any fruit, this sugar made from ground, dried dates is only moderately sweet.

Maple Sugar

· Maple sugar is made from maple syrup that has been boiled down to a sugary state, then dehydrated. It is very, very sweet.

Sucanat

· Sucanat stands for "sugar cane natural." It's the closest thing to "natural" sugar. It is sugar cane juice in a granulated form. Unlike nutritionally deficient table sugar, Sucanat retains all the sugar cane's vitamins and minerals.

· Sucanat has the same sweetening power as granulated sugar. 1 tablespoon sugar = 1 tablespoon Sucanat.

Honey

· Honeys vary widely in their sweetness. They range from 1½ times sweeter than table sugar all the way down to less sweet than table sugar.

· When replacing sugar with honey, start with a guideline of 1 tablespoon sugar = 2 teaspoons honey, then adjust to suit your taste if the honey you're using isn't particularly sweet.

· Honey does an even better job of preserving a bread's moisture than table sugar. In fact, because of its moisture-attracting properties, on humid days any breads containing honey will actually absorb moisture from the air.

· The darker the honey, the stronger and more acidic the taste.

· Honey will contribute some acid to your bread doughs.

· With age and cool temperatures, honey will eventually crystallize. To return it to its liquid state temporarily, you can either place it in a pan of hot water or warm it briefly in the microwave.

· Along the same lines, on cold winter days when the honey is so thick it will hardly budge, or when you're down to the bottom of the jar and want to capture every last drop, place your container of honey in the microwave (or in a pan of hot water) to warm it up and make it easier to pour. The average jar of honey will warm up in just 20 or 30 seconds on HIGH in the microwave. (For the "dregs," about 5 seconds should do it.)

· Store honey in a cool, dry, dark place. Keep tightly covered.

· If raw, unpasteurized honey is left exposed to the air, on humid days it will absorb water. If it absorbs a great deal of water, yeasts will grow and spoil it, turning its sugar into alcohol and carbon dioxide.

· If using raw, unpasteurized honey, it's best to heat it first (no higher than 180°F) to destroy the enzymes in it that may play havoc with your bread dough.

· We think proper homage should be paid to the incredible honey bee. Each bee works **an entire lifetime** just to produce one teaspoon of honey! So, please include the tiny honey bee next time you offer up high praise for that marvelous loaf of honey wheat bread you just enjoyed. What a gift!

Molasses

· During processing, sugar is spun in large centrifuges. The liquid that is spun out is boiled several times and yields different grades of molasses.

· Molasses is not as sweet as granulated sugar; 1 tablespoon sugar = 4 teaspoons molasses.

· Molasses will increase the acid level in your bread dough. To neutralize it, you can add a pinch of baking soda, if desired. (Since yeast prefers an acidic environment, we suggest you first try the recipe without the added baking soda.)

· We recommend the milder-flavored unsulphured variety of molasses.

· The shelf life of an opened jar of molasses is one year.

Maple Syrup

· The sap from maple trees is boiled down to a syrup state.

· Maple syrup is sweeter than granulated sugar but not as sweet as most honeys. 1 tablespoon sugar = ¾ tablespoon maple syrup.

· The lighter the color, the better the grade of maple syrup.

· Once opened, maple syrup should be stored in the refrigerator to inhibit the growth of any mold on top.

· If a mold develops, don't panic. Simply pour it off, strain the syrup through a sieve lined with cheesecloth, then bring it to a boil on the stove or in the microwave before pouring it back into the bottle.

Sorghum

· This syrup is similar to molasses but thinner and not as sweet.

· Sorghum is not a byproduct of sugar refining; rather, it is derived from crushing the stalks of the sorghum plant, then boiling down its juices.

Corn Syrup

· This is a sweet syrup that is made from the starch in corn. When used in breads, it helps keep them fresh and moist.

· Corn syrup has only half the sweetness of sugar: 1 tablespoon sugar = 2 tablespoons corn syrup.

Barley Malt Syrup

· Barley malt syrup is a complex sugar made from sprouted barley. It tastes like a cross between honey and molasses.

· Its sugar profile is 77% maltose, 15% glucose, 7% sucrose, and 1% fructose.

· The jar we use states that you can substitute barley malt syrup one to one for honey or molasses. In our bread baking, however, we found better results using half that amount. In other words: 1 tablespoon honey = ½ tablespoon (1½ teaspoons) barley malt syrup.

· "Hop-flavored" barley malt syrup is sold for brewing and is quite bitter tasting, not something you'd want to add to your breads as a sweetener.

· Barley malt syrup has been heated in processing so it contains none of the active malt enzymes found in diastatic malt powder (see "Dough Enhancers" on page 53) that would alter the chemistry of your bread baking.

· Once opened, store barley malt syrup in the refrigerator.

BROWN RICE SYRUP

· This thick, mild-tasting syrup is a product of fermented brown rice. You can use it as you would barley malt syrup.

· Rice syrup has a high proportion of complex carbohydrates; it does not enter the bloodstream as rapidly as simple sugars.

LIQUID FRUIT CONCENTRATES

· Products such as Fruit Sweet (pear, peach, and pineapple juice concentrates) and Fruit Source (grape juice concentrate and rice syrup) can be used to sweeten your breads. They contain no refined sugars.

STORAGE

· All sugars should be stored in airtight containers. They are hygroscopic (moisture-attracting) and will absorb water from the air.

EGGS

· Eggs add liquid, color, structure, nutrients, flavor, and tenderness to breads.

· Each large egg is equivalent to a scant ¼ cup liquid.

· Brown or white eggs can be used.

· If you have a bread that's a reluctant riser, replace ¼ cup of the liquid with a large egg.

· Breads containing eggs have a tendency to dry out faster than other breads. Adding extra fat to the recipe compensates for this tendency.

· To bring an egg to room temperature quickly, submerge it in hot tap water for a few moments.

· You can test an egg's freshness by submerging it in a pan of water. If it floats, it's not fresh.

GLUTEN

The term "gluten" can be confusing. In a bread machine cookbook it may refer to the elastic structure that is developed by kneading dough well, the protein content of the flour, or the additive included in some recipes to give certain breads more structure or to help them rise higher. We hope to clear up some of the confusion for you.

· While we tend to refer to the protein in wheat flour as gluten, technically there are four proteins: albumin, globulin, gliadin, and glutenin. When wheat flour is mixed with water and then kneaded, the gliadin and glutenin combine with the water to form an elastic, weblike structure called gluten. At first the long gluten fibers are very tangled, but in time, with proper kneading, those strands unfold, elongate, and begin to bond side by side. This gives the dough its weblike structure, its strength, smooth surface, texture, and elasticity.

· Gluten development is an essential element in almost all yeast breads. Those flours that are low in gliadin and glutenin such as rye, barley, buckwheat, millet, etc., need to be combined with a high percentage of wheat flour to produce an adequate gluten framework for baking.

· "High-gluten flour" or "gluten flour" in bins usually refers to a bread flour with 12 to 14 percent protein content. To be sure, ask first before purchasing.

· Vital wheat gluten refers to a product that is almost 100 percent pure gluten. It is isolated and removed from a wheat flour dough in a long process that involves washing the starch out of the flour. It is then dried, ground, packaged, and sold as vital wheat gluten.

· Vital wheat gluten is not a flour. It is an additive that gives the bread more structure, strength, and height. It is especially useful when baking whole grain breads that are low in gluten.

· In our recipes, when we list gluten as an optional ingredient, this is what we are referring to . . . vital wheat gluten.

· The producers of this gluten recommend using 1 teaspoon vital wheat gluten per cup of flour in white breads and 1½ teaspoons per cup of flour in whole-grain breads. We find doubling that amount for whole-grain breads works best in the bread machine. We rarely need to add any for white breads.

· Gluten absorbs water. When adding vital wheat gluten to your bread, observe the dough while it mixes and add more liquid, if needed.

· Vital wheat gluten's shelf life, stored unopened at room temperature, is two years. Opened, it will last about a year when kept in the refrigerator or freezer.

Dough Enhancers

Dough "enhancers" are optional supplements that can increase gluten strength, aid the yeast's fermentation, produce a more yeast-friendly environment, convert starch into sugar, or help emulsify oils. Their use will often result in taller, lighter loaves and/or breads that will stay fresher longer.

Most dough enhancers contain all-natural ingredients but there are a few that contain artificial ingredients. It's fun to experiment with them, but if your main purpose in owning a bread machine is to escape the chemically laden commercial breads, adding some of these extras to your homemade breads just doesn't make sense. Frankly, fresh home-baked bread seldom needs anything more than extra gluten once in a while. Don't mess with a good thing!

Gluten

· Companies such as Arrowhead Mills and Bob's Red Mill package and sell vital wheat gluten and vital wheat gluten flour. Some health food stores also sell it in their bulk bins.

· To create taller, lighter breads you can add gluten to your dough. It's most often used in whole-grain breads, which tend to bake up small and dense in the bread machine.

· See above for recommended amounts.

Diastatic Malt Powder (Malted Barley Flour)

· Malted barley or wheat powder is created from sprouted wheat or barley kernels that have been roasted, ground, filtered, and then dehydrated.

· Diastatic malt powder (dimalt) contains enzymes that break down the flour's starch and convert it into sugar (food for the yeast).

· It improves the bread's flavor, gives it a better texture, and helps it stay fresh longer.

· Adding this all-natural product makes it possible to reduce or eliminate the use of sugar in bread recipes.

· It should be used in small quantities: Start by replacing each tablespoon of sugar with ½ teaspoon diastatic malt. You can increase it by ¼ teaspoon each time you try a certain recipe until you notice your dough developing gummy spots, then cut back the quantity. A few experimental tries and you will find the right amount for your breads.

· If you add too little, the bread will be a sickly pale color. Add too much and the dough will turn very sticky and not bake up properly.

· Since diastatic malt continues to convert starch into sugar during rising, do not use it in any long-rising breads such as French or sourdough.

· If you're interested in a challenge, you can create your own diastatic barley or wheat malt. *The Laurel's Kitchen Bread Book,* by Laurel Robertson (New York: Random House, 1984), gives full directions for sprouting, drying, and producing your own diastatic malt on pages 274 and 275. (You do need some type of grain grinder to mill the dried sprouts.)

· If your health food store doesn't carry diastatic malt powder, try one of the companies listed in our Sources section (page 215).

· It keeps well in the freezer.

LECITHIN

· Lecithin, an emulsifier that will delay the staling process in breads, is available in granular or liquid form.

· Lecithin is found naturally in egg yolks and soy beans.

· One tablespoon of lecithin granules contains 50 calories.

· We've done numerous tests using lecithin and it's been our experience that when combined with additional gluten, lecithin seems to enhance gluten's power to give added height to breads. Those breads with both gluten and lecithin added were measurably taller than those made with just gluten. Breads baked with added lecithin but no extra gluten were no different from breads baked without either lecithin or gluten. Our bottom line: Lecithin and gluten combined produced the highest loaves. Lecithin by itself, while it may have added to the keeping quality of the bread, did not increase the height of the bread.

· Use ¼ teaspoon lecithin (granular or liquid) per cup of flour.

· If you use liquid lecithin, which is very sticky, it helps to oil the measuring spoon first.

ASCORBIC ACID (VITAMIN C)

· Ascorbic acid strengthens the protein in flour and gives the loaf more volume.
· Some bread flours contain either potassium bromate or ascorbic acid to give added strength to the dough.
· Testing that we have done using 150 mg ascorbic acid per cup of flour has resulted in much higher loaves of bread.
· You can purchase pure vitamin C (ascorbic acid) in crystal, tablet, or capsule form at any well-stocked pharmacy or health food store.
· It will require a little bit of math on your part to calculate how much of the crystals, crushed tablet, or capsule contents you will need to equal 150 mg. For instance, we purchased a jar of vitamin C crystals that contained 5,000 mg pure vitamin C per teaspoon. To reduce it down to a 150 mg amount, we had to use ⅟₃₂ of a teaspoon! It hardly seems possible that such a minute amount can make any difference in the size of the bread, but it does.

POTASSIUM BROMATE

· Bread flour with this additive is known as "bromated" flour.
· Potassium bromate is added to some bread flours to give the gluten added strength, which in turn will result in taller, lighter loaves of bread.
· Some studies indicate that potassium bromate is carcinogenic. In California, any flour containing potassium bromate must have a health warning included.
· Ascorbic acid can be used in place of potassium bromate.

COMMERCIAL DOUGH ENHANCERS

· There is a commercial dough enhancer on the market that contains a little bit of everything: whey, soy lecithin, tofu, citric acid, yeast, sea salt, natural spice blend, cornstarch, ascorbic acid. On the container, the recommended amount is 1 teaspoon per cup of flour. We have not tried this product (its name is "Dough Enhancer"), yet know others who are pleased with the results.
· If you can't find Dough Enhancer in your stores, Magic Mill sells it directly (see Sources, page 215).

· There are also products, such as S500, that commercial bakeries use to enhance breads. Some may eventually find their way to the retail market as more and more of us bake our own breads.

SOURDOUGH

A sourdough starter is the "sour" in sourdough. It's basically a combination of flour, liquid, and yeast stored in a loosely covered jar or crock in the refrigerator. Frequent use or regular feeding keeps it alive. Some starters have been known to survive for generations!

There are probably as many sourdough starter recipes as there are wrinkles on an elephant. We won't go into them here, but we encourage you to find a good sourdough cookbook and try a few of the different types. For now, we'd simply like to offer a few tips and facts we've learned from our baking.

USING A STARTER

· Bring refrigerated starter to room temperature before using it. You can place it in a bowl of warm water if you're in a hurry or you can leave it out overnight if you plan to use it in the morning.

· Like most things in life, sourdough starter gets better with age. So don't be discouraged if your first breads don't quite live up to your sourest expectations. Just keep baking with it and very soon you'll notice it taking on its own tangy personality.

· Experiment. Use your sourdough starter in some of your favorite recipes. Rye breads are especially yummy when soured. If your starter is roughly half liquid and half flour, when you add starter to a recipe, consider half the amount of starter used as liquid and reduce the liquid in the recipe by that amount. In other words, if you choose to add 1 cup sourdough starter to a rye bread recipe that lists 1¼ cups water, count the 1 cup starter as ½ cup liquid and deduct that amount from your 1¼ cups water. (For that recipe your liquids would be 1 cup sourdough starter and ¾ cup water.)

· After each use, the starter needs to be replenished with equal amounts of liquid and flour. Do so, then cover it loosely and leave it out at room temperature for several hours until it increases and turns spongy-looking. Stir it down, then refrigerate.

· Your starter should always be kept in the refrigerator or freezer. The exceptions: those first few days as it's developing, the few hours before it's used, and the few hours after it's replenished or fed.

· Feed your starter once a month if you are not using it. Add equal amounts of flour and warm liquid (90° to 100°F). Cover loosely and allow it to stand in a warm location (70° to 95°F) until it expands and turns spongy-looking. Stir it down and then place it in the refrigerator, loosely covered.

· Remove the starter from its container every so often and give the container a good wash job in hot water.

· Sourdough starter ages best when handled with tender, loving care (don't we all!). So, do remember to feed it. If you're going to be gone or know you won't be baking with your starter for an extended period of time, you can freeze it. When you choose to use it again, allow your starter to sit at room temperature for 24 hours to thaw out and come back to life.

· If you'd like to make a "backup" of your starter for safekeeping or share it with friends across the country, consider dehydrating some of it. Here's how: Spoon enough starter on foam-type paper plates or large wax-paper—lined trays to coat the entire surface with a thin layer of starter. A thin coating will dry completely in approximately 24 hours. Once thoroughly dry, lift it off in large pieces and place it in a food processor, blender, or grain mill. Process briefly until coarsely ground. Store in a glass jar or plastic bag someplace cool. When you are ready to rehydrate your dried starter, place ½ cup warm water (90° to 100°F) in a 1½-quart glass or ceramic container. Add ¼ cup ground starter and then ¼ cup flour. Stir well with a wooden spoon. Place container in a warm location (between 75° and 95°F) and within several hours your starter should show signs of life with surface bubbles. At that point, add another ½ cup warm water and ½ cup more flour, stir, and allow the starter to feed overnight at room temperature before you use it or loosely cover it and store it in your refrigerator for later use.

· If, after freezing or several weeks of nonuse, your starter looks a little sluggish and isn't displaying its usual bubbly personality, reserve 1 or 2 tablespoons of the starter in a separate bowl and pour the rest away. Thoroughly wash the container and place the reserved starter back into the clean container. Add 1 cup warm liquid (90° to 100°F) and 1 cup flour. Cover loosely and let it stand in a warm place (70° to 95°F) for several hours until bubbly and a clear liquid begins to form on top. You may need to repeat this process once or twice to bring it back to its bubbly, sour-smelling self again.

· To maintain a 70° to 95°F temperature for your starter, place it in any warm location such as an oven with a pilot light on, a warm kitchen, on top of the water heater or refrigerator, in the sunshine during the day, in a bowl filled with water set on a warming tray, or directly on a heating pad. We've even heard of people placing starter or rising dough in a warm car. That sounds like a great idea until the one time you forget all about it and it bubbles out all over the upholstery! Try explaining that sour odor every time it's your turn to drive in the car pool.

How to Make the Sourest Sourdough

· Remove your starter from the refrigerator and bring it up to room temperature.

· Combine the amount of starter called for in your recipe with the liquid and two-thirds of the flour.

· Stir, cover the bowl, and allow it to sit at room temperature for at least 24 hours.

· Combine this mixture in your bread machine pan with the remaining ingredients in the recipe.

· Potato starters are usually sweeter starters. Those made with skim milk and yogurt are the sourest.

Miscellaneous Facts and Helpful Hints

· Use only wooden utensils and glass or ceramic containers. The starter will corrode metal.

· The grayish or yellowish liquid that rises to the top is the "hooch." Just stir it back in before using your starter.

· Do not keep your starter in a container that is tightly sealed. The accumulating gasses could shatter the jar.

· If you just don't seem to have the knack for getting a starter started, don't despair. Nobody's going to show up on your doorstep pointing fingers and snickering at you. The world doesn't even have to know. Instead, just tiptoe down to your favorite gourmet cooking store and pick up a packet of instant sourdough starter. Mix it up as directed and you'll be in sourdough heaven in no time!

· You can use your sourdough starter to create sublime pancakes and waffles, too.

WHEN TO DISCARD YOUR STARTER

· If your starter turns pink or orange or develops mold, discard it and start again.

· If you neglected your starter for months on end, tried to resuscitate it but to no avail, it's time to bid it adieu and start over.

We hate to be the bearer of bad news, but if you had your heart set on duplicating the incredible sourdoughs of San Francisco fame, you can forget it. To begin with, you'd have to have a starter that was an offspring of theirs. When was the last time you saw any of the famous bakeries handing out starter samples? Then you'd actually have to live in the Bay Area to capture the same airborne yeasts, use the same water, and duplicate the remaining ingredients. But pick your chin up off the ground. You can still create a little slice of heaven with your very own sourdough ingredients!

MISCELLANEOUS INGREDIENTS

CARAMEL COLORING

· This is added to pumpernickels, black breads, and some European peasant breads to give them their characteristic dark color.

· It's simple to make and even simpler to buy (in its concentrated form from a bakery).

· **Caution: Read the entire directions before you begin!**

In a small, very heavy saucepan, combine ½ cup sugar and 2 tablespoons water. Bring mixture to a boil over medium heat; let boil for about 15 minutes, stirring frequently with a wooden spoon. (Don't be alarmed. It will harden, remelt, and smoke during this process.) Remove pan from heat when the mixture turns a very dark molasses color. **VERY IMPORTANT: ALLOW THE MIXTURE TO COOL COMPLETELY (10 MINUTES) BEFORE ADDING MORE WATER. YOU WILL AVOID AN EXPLOSIVE SITUATION THAT COULD LEAVE YOU BADLY BURNED.** (At this point, you may think you've ruined your pan because the sugar is now a very thick glob in the bottom of it. Have faith. Keep going.) When the mixture is cool, add ¼ cup boiling water. Return the pan to the stove, stir over medium heat for about 5 minutes until it becomes a smooth, thin liquid. Cool completely; store in a covered jar at room temperature indefinitely. Add 1 tablespoon caramel coloring to your bread doughs to give them a dark color (it won't add sweetness). You can also brush it on pumpernickel and black breads as a glaze before baking them in the oven.

CHILE PEPPERS

· If you like your chiles on the mild side, select fresh Anaheim chiles. They are the long, tapered, green chiles in the produce section. You can also buy mild green chiles in a can.

· For lovers of the hot and spicy variety, choose either fresh or canned jalapeños. They are small, dark green chiles.

· Hotter still are serrano chiles. They are dark green, smaller and thinner than the jalapeño peppers.

· The chile pepper's "heat" is in the seeds and ribs. Since canned diced jalapeños include the seeds and ribs, we found they produced a hotter bread than the fresh jalapeño peppers with seeds and ribs removed.

· When working with chile peppers, avoid touching your face, eyes, or mouth. Wash your hands well when done. If you have sensitive skin, wear rubber gloves.

· **A general rule of thumb:** "The smaller the chile, the hotter the fire." Keep that in mind the next time you're in a Mexican restaurant and a friend dares you to munch on that *tiny* little chile pepper.

DAIRY PRODUCTS

· We've discovered that several products vary greatly in density, texture, acidity levels, etc., from brand to brand and from one part of the country to another. These items include sour cream, cottage cheese, buttermilk, ricotta cheese, yogurt, and applesauce. After a trip to the east coast, Lois learned that the sour cream her sons and their families were using in their breads was twice as thick as the brand she used. It made a big difference in the final results. Buttermilk varies widely, too, as we learned from the network of bread bakers on a computer bulletin board who tested our DeDe's Buttermilk Bread. They ended up with tall loaves, tiny loaves, and everything in between. The different brands of buttermilk (liquid and powder) with their varying levels of acidity seemed to be the culprit. So, if you're having trouble duplicating a particular bread, there's a possibility it's a variation in the composition of the ingredients that's at fault.

FRUIT

· When a recipe calls for ripe bananas, make sure they are very ripe. They should have dark spots on the peel. If they are not ripe, they won't mash up properly and provide the necessary "liquid."

· Adding fruit, with its natural pectin, will improve the keeping quality of your breads.

· To help keep fragile fruits such as berries intact, freeze them first. Spread them out on a baking sheet and freeze them individually. Once frozen, place them in a plastic bag or container until needed. Add them to the bread dough in their frozen state.

· If you have a dehydrator or convection oven, try drying your fruits first. They will hold up better in the dough and give a more intense flavor.

· If you add dried fruits, you may also need to increase the liquid slightly.

· Before squeezing the juice from a fresh orange or lemon, remove the zest first either by grating or with a vegetable peeler and then chopping it up in a small food processor. Freeze the peel to have on hand when you want to add a little zip to a particular bread.

· When removing the zest of any citrus fruit, remove only the colored outer skin. The white pith underneath is bitter and not desirable.

· Heat lemons and oranges briefly in the microwave before squeezing. They'll produce more juice.

Nuts

· Almonds, brazil nuts, filberts, peanuts, pecans, pine nuts, and walnuts are wonderful additions to homemade breads, especially fruit breads.

· Pecans and filberts add their own extra sweetness while walnuts have a more bitter flavor, which balances well with the sweetest fruit breads.

· Nuts contain natural oils that will turn rancid when stored at warm temperatures for any length of time. To preserve their freshness, store them in the refrigerator or freezer. A few rancid nuts can ruin your perfect loaf.

· Toasting nuts and seeds on a cookie sheet in a 350°F oven for 8 to 10 minutes will bring out their flavors. Watch them carefully to avoid scorching.

Packaged Bread Machine Mixes

· We've tried a few of the packaged mixes now on the market and though they aren't quite as wonderful tasting as what you can make with your own fresh ingredients, they are certainly acceptable and can have a place in the bread machine baker's pantry. Their best features: most bake up beautifully (we tried them in several different machines), they're incredibly convenient (all you do is add water and the packet of yeast), and they are ideal for the Delayed-Bake Cycle. For those reasons, we think they'd be perfect as part of a starter kit for the brand-new bread machine owner. Producing nice-looking loaves of bread the first few times would instill some confidence in the hesitant bread baker, plus encourage the new owner to use different cycles on his or her machine. For the experienced bread baker, the mixes are handy to have around for those moments when 30 seconds before dashing out the door in the morning is about all the time you can allocate for baking your daily loaf of bread.

Potatoes

· Potatoes, either instant or freshly mashed, are a boon to homemade breads. They add moisture, a naturally sweet, rich flavor, and seem to give the yeast a boost, as well.

· We have added up to ½ cup of plain mashed potatoes in some recipes. Prepared mashed potatoes contain a great deal of moisture so when you add them to your recipes, reduce your liquids by at least ¼ cup to start. If the dough appears dry, add more liquid 1 tablespoon at a time while it's kneading.

RAISINS

· For added flavor, soak raisins in vanilla, rum, brandy, or dust with cinnamon before adding them to a recipe.

· You can store them in the refrigerator. Cold raisins will hold up better during the kneading process.

SEEDS

· Caraway, poppy, sesame, and sunflower seeds are the most popular seeds used in bread baking. Though millet is actually a grain, it can be added to breads as a seed.

· We prefer the raw, unsalted sunflower seeds from the bins at out local health food store. They have a mild, sweet flavor. If you can locate only the toasted, salted variety, reduce the amount of salt in your recipe.

· Seeds, like nuts, contain natural oils that will turn rancid quickly if exposed to warm temperatures. It is best to store them in the refrigerator or freezer to prevent rancidity.

· Toasting millet, sesame, and sunflower seeds in a nonstick skillet over medium heat for a few minutes will accentuate their flavor. Watch closely to ensure they don't burn and turn bitter.

TOXIC SPICES

· Brown and golden spices such as cinnamon, nutmeg, cloves, cardamom, mace, allspice, ginger, and mustard contain compounds which are toxic to yeast. Limit their amount to a scant ½ teaspoon per cup of flour. If you prefer a stronger cinnamon or spice flavor, use it in a filling or a topping.

SUBSTITUTIONS

BREAD FLOUR

· To create your own bread flour, place 1½ teaspoons vital wheat gluten in a 1-cup measuring cup and then fill with all-purpose flour.

BUTTERMILK

· To create a mock buttermilk, add 1 tablespoon lemon juice or distilled white vinegar to 1 cup warm nonfat or low-fat milk. Stir and let the mixture clabber for about 5 minutes.

· Replace the buttermilk with water and add 1 tablespoon powdered buttermilk to the dry ingredients for every ¼ cup buttermilk you are replacing. For example, if the recipe calls for ¾ cup buttermilk, replace it with ¾ cup water and add 3 tablespoons buttermilk powder to the dry ingredients. (**Note:** When substituting powdered buttermilk in a recipe, omit the baking soda if it is a listed ingredient. The powder is less acidic than fresh buttermilk and the baking soda further neutralizes it—not a desirable goal when working with yeast.)

· Substitute plain yogurt in equal measure for buttermilk.

EGGS

· There are many low- and non-cholesterol egg substitutes in the milk and freezer sections of grocery stores today. (They do contain eggs.) Add a scant ¼ cup of those products to replace one large egg in a recipe.

· Two egg whites equal one whole egg.

· For each large egg, substitute 3 tablespoons water and 2 teaspoons Ener-G Egg Replacer (powdered non-egg product).

· You can omit eggs in recipes by replacing each with a scant ¼ cup of water.

FATS

· Replace fats in bread recipes with an equal amount of unsweetened applesauce, or any other puréed fruit, and reduce the recipe's liquid by an equal amount.

· In some recipes you can omit the fat without replacement.

· Butter, margarine, oil, and solid shortening can be used interchangeably in most recipes. If you substitute a liquid for a solid, observe the dough as it's mixing. If it looks too wet, add 1 to 2 tablespoons more flour as needed.

· Products such as Wonderslim replace fat with all-natural products such as water and dried plums. For every tablespoon of fat in the recipe, use ½ tablespoon (1½ teaspoons) Wonderslim. You can find Wonderslim in major grocery stores, usually near the sugar substitutes.

FRUITS AND VEGETABLES

· If you decide to add fresh fruit or vegetables to a recipe, as a general rule of thumb consider them to be half liquid and deduct that amount of liquid from your recipe. Adding 1 cup chopped apples means reducing the liquid in the recipe by ½ cup. Observe the dough as it mixes and adjust the balance by adding either more liquid or more flour, 1 tablespoon at a time, as needed.

HERBS

· When substituting fresh for dried herbs, triple the amount. 1 tablespoon dried herbs equals 3 tablespoons fresh.

MILK

· You may use any milk interchangeably: whole, low-fat, 1 percent, or skim.

· Replace the milk with water and add ¾ to 1 tablespoon nonfat dry milk to the dry ingredients for every ¼ cup milk you are replacing.

· Non-dairy milk products such as soy milk, rice milk, etc., may be used in equal measure to replace milk in recipes.

· Powdered soy milk or tofu milk powder may be used instead of nonfat dry milk; follow the package directions.

· Equal measures of vegetable cooking water, fruit juices, vegetable juices, flat beer, and just plain water are all viable substitutions for milk in most recipes. Use your best judgment when combining various flavors, but don't hesitate to experiment.

ONION

· You can substitute 1 tablespoon dried onion flakes for ¼ cup chopped fresh onion. You will also need to add 1 to 2 tablespoons water for every ¼ cup chopped fresh onion omitted. Observe the dough while it is mixing and add the water as needed.

SALT

· So far, there is no salt substitute that has the right properties for use in baking breads.

· A "lite" salt must contain both potassium chloride and sodium; plain potassium chloride will not work. Morton Lite Salt is the only brand we've been able to locate so far that fits the bill. Use it measure for measure in your bread recipes.

· You can use either table salt or sea salt in bread recipes.

· If you prefer to use coarse kosher salt, increase the amount by 1 teaspoon to allow for its coarser texture.

· DO NOT use rock salt as a substitute for coarse kosher salt. It is meant for ice cream makers and paved highways, not our tummies.

SOUR CREAM

· Replace all or part of whole sour cream with plain yogurt, reduced-fat sour cream, or fat-free sour cream.

· To make a mock low-fat sour cream: In a blender or food processor, combine 1 cup low-fat cottage cheese, ¼ cup buttermilk or plain yogurt, and 1 tablespoon lemon juice. Blend for a few seconds.

SOURDOUGH

· If you want to add sourdough starter to a recipe, count half of it as liquid and deduct that amount from the liquid listed in the recipe. If you use 1 cup starter, reduce the liquid in the recipe by ½ cup.

SUGAR

· For a different flavor, you can substitute an equal measure of brown sugar for white. (Brown sugar should always be packed firmly into the measuring spoon or cup when it is measured.)
· Do not substitute powdered sugar for table sugar.
· One tablespoon of granulated white sugar equals the following:

1 packed tablespoon of brown sugar
A heaping 1 ½ teaspoons fructose
1 tablespoon turbinado sugar
1 tablespoon Sucanat
2 teaspoons honey
4 teaspoons molasses
2 tablespoons corn syrup
¾ tablespoon maple syrup

· Other substitutes for table sugar include: sorghum, maple sugar, date sugar, barley malt syrup, brown rice syrup, pureed fruits, frozen fruit concentrates, Fruit Sweet, jams and jellies.
· As of this writing, Sweet One and Sugar Twin are the only sugar substitutes in the grocery stores that can be used in baking. Each packet is equivalent to 2 teaspoons sugar; however, we found that using the full amount of Sugar Twin produced too sweet a loaf for our tastes. If you, like us, prefer your bread less sweet, use half the recommended amount of Sugar Twin.
· You can omit the sugar in most recipes and replace it with diastatic malt powder. You use much less malt powder than sugar. Our best test results were achieved by substituting ½ teaspoon malt powder for each tablespoon of sweetener.

WHOLE WHEAT FLOUR

· If you have no whole wheat flour on hand, you can create your own. In the bottom of a measuring cup (for dry ingredients), place 1 teaspoon wheat germ and 2½ tablespoons wheat bran. Fill the cup with unbleached wheat flour and level.

WHOLE WHEAT BREAD FLOUR

· To create "homemade" whole wheat bread flour, follow the preceding directions for whole wheat flour but replace the unbleached flour with bread flour.

YEAST

· One ¼-ounce packet of yeast equals 2¼ teaspoons yeast.
· One ⅗-ounce cake of compressed yeast is equal to one ¼-ounce packet active dry yeast.

4

How to Adjust Recipes to Fit Your Dietary Needs

THE NUTRITIONAL
BENEFITS OF HOMEMADE BREAD

We're always amazed when people make the remark, "Oh, I can't buy a bread machine. I'd end up eating too much bread!" Has anybody checked out the new USDA Food Guide Pyramid lately? The Basic Four Food Groups are a thing of the past. The foundation of this healthier eating guideline is the bread, cereal, rice, and pasta group—six to eleven servings daily! Haven't we all known it for years . . . we consume too many high-fat meat and dairy products and not nearly enough grains, fruits, and vegetables? Breathes there a soul who isn't aware it's time to trim the fat? That means it's time to rethink some lifelong bad habits. Instead of being the main portion of our meals, meat and dairy products should be used as supplements to meals centered around grains, beans, fruits, and vegetables. And any healthy vegetarian will chime in that it's possible to do without meat entirely (and dairy if you're a vegan)!

Much like the baked potato, bread is often maligned as being fattening. It's not the bread that's fattening, it's what you put on it! An entire 1½-pound loaf of whole wheat bread might contain only 1¼ tablespoons of fat, 1½ tablespoons of sugar, 3 cups of flour, and an egg or a cup of lowfat milk . . . not too bad when you divide that by 12 or 14 slices. In fact, for those of us who have been up and down the scale like a yo-yo, wholesome bread can be a newfound "friend." If you ask the waiter to remove the bread basket in a restaurant; if you remove the top half of the bun before eating a hamburger; if you eat your sandwiches open-faced in an effort to cut calories, it may be time to rethink your tactics. Filling up on the wonderful breads and rolls many restaurants now serve (sans butter, of course) can certainly take the edge off your appetite. By the time your higher-calorie, higher-fat entrée appears, you're much less likely to overindulge. In fact, it's quite possible to dine out and be very satisfied with good bread, a dinner salad, and a light appetizer rather than a full-course meal. As for eating burgers or sandwiches open-faced, a wiser move is to reduce the size of the hamburger patty and to make your sandwiches with thick slices of whole-grain bread and very little meat filling. You'll get all the flavor, more satiety, less fat, and fewer calories.

If you have other special dietary requirements, it's possible to adjust the bread recipes to better suit your nutritional needs. In this section we will give you plenty of tips on how to reduce or eliminate fat, sugar, salt, cholesterol, and animal and dairy products in your daily bread. There are also computer software programs that will provide a nutritional analysis of your recipes. This may be a useful aid for those of you who closely monitor your meals.

Do you recall how we described gluten as being an essential ingredient in the bread-baking process? In this chapter we have to modify that statement. People with wheat and gluten intolerances are baking gluten-free breads all the time in their bread machines! That came as quite a shock to us. Only a few months ago we would have dismissed it as impossible. We hope this news will reach others with the same condition and open new doors for them. Until now they've been faced with paying premium prices for their gluten-free breads.

So, the good news is, people with heart conditions, weight problems, diabetes, high cholesterol, celiac sprue, wheat allergies, lactose intolerance, and those who choose not to eat dairy or animal products can still enjoy great, wholesome, preservative-free breads from their bread machines without tremendous cost or major effort. Bread is good for you! To the person who's afraid to buy a bread machine and exclaims, "I'd end up eating too much bread," we say, "GREAT!"

WAYS TO REDUCE OR ELIMINATE FATS IN BREAD

· You can replace the fat in most loaves with an equal measure of unsweetened applesauce. Diana Lewis, a friend of ours, has this suggestion: Freeze your applesauce in 1-tablespoon quantities in ice-cube trays. Once frozen, pop them into a heavy plastic bag and store them in the freezer until needed.

· Instead of applesauce, you can use any other unsweetened fruit you have on hand. Simply purée it in a blender or food processor. **Note:** When testing applesauce and puréed fruit as replacements for solid fats such as butter, margarine, or shortening, we noticed that our breads had better texture when we reduced the liquid in the recipes by the same amount. In other words, when we replaced 2 tablespoons of butter with 2 tablespoons of applesauce, our breads were coarse textured and chewy. When we made that same substitution but also reduced the liquid in the recipe by 2 tablespoons, our bread was much finer textured and very similar to the original recipe.

· We've also discovered that you can simply omit the fat in many recipes without any replacement. Of course, those breads are not as tender and turn stale quickly.

· Light margarine may be used in place of regular margarine. It contains more water than regular margarine so you may need to reduce the liquids by a few teaspoons if you find your breads have a coarser texture when using light margarine.

· Fat-substitute products such as Wonderslim contain all-natural ingredients such as water and dried plums. The direction say to replace the fat in the recipe with one half the amount of Wonderslim.

· Another ingredient in your bread that contains fat is milk. By substituting nonfat milk, fruit juices, or vegetable juices for whole milk you've eliminated another source of fat.

· If a recipe calls for sour cream, consider plain yogurt as a substitute. There are also reduced-fat and fat-free sour creams that perform equally well.

· Egg substitutes found in the milk or freezer section of the grocery store are lower in fat than whole fresh eggs. Replacing one whole egg with two egg whites is another option. If you want to eliminate eggs altogether, there's a product called Ener-G Egg Replacer that has worked well in all the breads we've tested. It's sold in health food stores or can be ordered directly from Ener-G (see Sources, page 215).

· Avoid such high-fat extras as nuts, cheese, sunflower seeds, bacon, cream cheese, and diced meats.

How to Reduce or Eliminate Sugar in Bread

· Some sweeteners have more sweetening power than granulated sugar, which means you can use less of them. These include: honey, fructose, barley malt syrup, maple syrup, and maple sugar. They also contain more nutrients than table sugar.

· Puréed fruits and frozen fruit concentrates offer a more acceptable alternative to refined sugar for some people. Reduce the liquids in the recipe by the amount of fruit added.

· There's also a product called Fruit Sweet (see Sources, page 215), which is free of any refined sugars. It is a liquid blend of concentrated pear, peach, and pineapple juices. We've noticed a similar product called Fruit Source at our health food store. It's a combination of grape juice concentrate and whole rice syrup. When using either of these to replace granulated sugar, reduce the liquid in the recipe by an equal amount.

· Commercial fructose is usually refined from table sugar or corn syrup, not fruit. Natural sources for fructose are fruits, vegetables, and honey.

· Barley malt syrup is a complex sugar made from sprouted barley. It falls somewhere between honey and molasses in flavor. It's comprised of 77% maltose, 15% glucose, 7% sucrose, and 1% fructose. When we used it as a substitute for honey, our results were best when we used half the amount. If the recipe called for 2 tablespoons honey, we used 1 tablespoon barley malt syrup.

· Similar to barley malt syrup is brown rice syrup, a product of fermented brown rice.

· There are a wide variety of sugar substitutes on the market but the only ones that will withstand the heat of baking without turning bitter are Sugar Twin and Sweet One. Nutrasweet has developed an encapsulated form that slowly releases its sweetener during cooking. The FDA is considering approval right now.

· Sugar Twin contains 1½ calories per teaspoon and its ingredients include dextrose, sodium, and saccharin. It comes in both brown and white "sugar" versions. Loaves tested with Sugar Twin using their suggested amounts proved to be much sweeter than we preferred. We suggest you experiment, too. We found that cutting the amount of sweetener in half produced a much more acceptable loaf for our palates.

· Sweet One contains 2 calories per teaspoon and its ingredient list includes dextrose, acesulfame K, and cream of tartar. Our test samples using Sweet One didn't seem overly sweet. Their suggested sugar equivalents worked well.

· To eliminate adding any sugar to your recipes, use diastatic malt powder instead. (See our Sources section on page 215 if you have trouble locating it.) It contains active enzymes extracted from sprouted barley that will convert some of the flour's starch into maltose, supplying the necessary sugar the yeast needs to thrive and multiply.

· Avoid adding extra sugars unwittingly by the use of such products as chocolate chips, jams, marmalade, some peanut butters, sweetened condensed milk, dates, etc.

· Diabetics should check with their doctors for information on the beneficial effects of a high-fiber diet. Studies have shown it slows down the absorption of carbohydrates into the system.

CUTTING THE SALT IN HALF

· Salt has an important role in bread baking: It inhibits the yeast's growth, strengthens the gluten, and brings out the wonderful flavors of the various ingredients. Omitting it altogether results in loaves that collapse during baking or never rise well to begin with; and in both cases they're very flat-tasting breads.

· It's easy to reduce the salt in most recipes; just a little experimenting on your part is needed. Start by reducing the amount in your recipe by ¼ teaspoon. If it's still an acceptable-looking loaf, next time try reducing the salt by another ¼ teaspoon.

· Items high in sodium include cheese, salted butter, margarine, bacon, ham, salami, pepperoni, pickles, V-8 and tomato juice, peanuts, salted sunflower seeds, softened water, and processed foods. If you want to keep the sodium count in your breads at a low level, avoid adding these ingredients to your dough.

· Any "lite" salt or salt substitute must contain some sodium to perform effectively in your bread doughs. Just plain potassium chloride will not interact properly with the yeast and developing gluten. Understandably, we were unable to locate any salt substitutes listing sodium as an ingredient. Morton Lite Salt, however, contains both sodium and potassium chloride. It contains half the sodium of regular table salt. Loaves we tested using this light salt as a replacement for the regular salt listed in the recipe were identical in size, shape, and texture to loaves baked with regular salt. (In case you're wondering, "Why even bother with the light salt? Why not just reduce the salt in the recipe by 50 percent?" We tested many loaves and in most cases, the breads with the light salt baked up better than those with half the amount of salt omitted.)

· Most of us should keep our sodium intake under 2,400 milligrams a day.

LOWERING THE CHOLESTEROL IN BREAD

· Animal fats equal cholesterol.

· To eliminate cholesterol in your daily bread, replace the animal fats such as butter, milk, egg yolks, sour cream, and cheese with healthier substitutions.

· Use nonfat milk rather than whole or low-fat milk.

· Select a buttermilk made with cultured nonfat milk rather than one made with low-fat milk.

· Use margarine instead of butter.

· Use vegetable oils such as canola, corn, soy, safflower, and olive oil to replace butter. (Canola oil is lower in saturated fats than any other oil.) Here is a comparison of the cholesterol and saturated fat content of most vegetable oils and shortenings:

	CHOLESTEROL	SATURATED FAT
Canola oil	0%	6%
Safflower oil	0%	9%
Sunflower oil	0%	11%
Corn oil	0%	13%
Peanut oil	0%	13%

Olive oil	0%	14%
Soybean oil	0%	15%
Cottonseed oil	0%	27%
Palm oil	0%	51%
Coconut oil	0%	77%
Margarine	0%	18%
Vegetable shortening	0%	26%
Butter	33%	54%

· Replace butter with an equal amount of puréed fruits, such as applesauce.

· Substitute 2 egg whites for 1 whole egg.

· Most liquid egg substitutes are cholesterol-free. You can find them in your grocer's freezer or dairy section. For each large egg, substitute a scant ¼ cup liquid egg substitute.

· Replace each egg with Ener-G Egg Replacer or a scant ¼ cup water.

· Replace whole sour cream with fat-free sour cream.

· Most low-fat cottage cheeses and yogurts are low in cholesterol. Check the labels before purchasing.

HIGH-FIBER BREADS

· With the introduction of more and more processed and refined foods, fast foods, and high-sugar, high-fat snack foods, our consumption of fiber declined during the 1900s. Breads, cereals, beans, fruits, and vegetables—the best sources of dietary fiber—were pushed aside. It's exciting to think that the bread machine may stop or at least slow down this trend!

· Unlike vitamins, minerals, and protein, fiber isn't considered an essential nutrient, but many studies show a link between high-fiber diets and a reduction in certain types of diseases and cancers.

· High-fiber diets are lower in calories, more filling, and less likely to contribute to weight gain than diets low in fiber and high in protein.

· The recommended amount of fiber adults should consume daily is between 20 and 35 grams.

· There are two types of fiber—soluble and insoluble—and they perform two different functions in our systems.

· Soluble fiber absorbs water in the stomach and intestine, and thus provides a feeling of satiety and slows the absorption of food. This makes soluble fiber an ally in the battle of the bulge as well as an aid to persons with hypoglycemia and diabetes. Studies have also found that insoluble fiber lowers cholesterol and triglyceride levels in the blood.

· Soluble fiber dissolves in water. It is found mainly in fruits, vegetables, dried beans, peas, lentils, barley, and unrefined oats.

· Insoluble fiber passes through our systems pretty much intact and is known for its laxative effect.

· The best sources for insoluble fiber are wheat bran and whole grains. Dried beans, peas, fruits, and vegetables also contain some insoluble fiber.

· Eating a wide variety of fiber-rich foods is more beneficial than suddenly adding ten slices of whole wheat bread to your diet. It's better to include both types of fiber in your diet, rather than focus on one or the other.

· The whole-grain breads such as whole wheat, oatmeal, bran, cracked wheat, pumpernickel, and the fruit and vegetable breads are certainly an easy, delicious way to add extra fiber to your menus. Start gradually by replacing some of the high-fat, high-sugar foods with high-fiber ones. You'll eventually make a very painless, healthful change in your eating habits!

· If you want to increase the fiber in your breads, add ⅓ to ½ cup oatmeal, oat bran, bulgur, cooked cracked wheat, sprouted grains, miller's bran, or multigrain cereals to your breads. Observe your dough as it is kneading because you will probably have to add 1 to 2 tablespoons extra liquid as well.

· Diced, raw fruits or vegetables are also fiber-rich additions you can make to your daily bread. In that case, when you add fruits or vegetables, you'll need to either reduce the liquids in your bread or add some extra flour while it mixes.

Breads for Animal Lovers

No, this segment isn't about creating special breads to take to the zoo or recipes for extra-special morsels to toss to the ducks and birds in your city park. The following helpful hints are meant for those of you with gentle spirits who choose to protect animals and their products rather than eat them. If you don't already know, it's possible, with just a few minor changes, to create wonderful breads that will suit your needs.

· When milk is used in a recipe, you can substitute an equal quantity of water, fruit juice, vegetable juice, or the water used for cooking vegetables or beans. (When using the liquid left after cooking beans, use no more than ½ cup or the result will be too rich.) There are also products made from soy or rice that are milklike in consistency and appearance. They include: Vita Soy, Fat-free Soy Moo, Edensoy, West Soy, Rice Dream, and probably many others in different parts of the country. (Be a label reader; some milklike beverages are much higher in fat than others.)

· If your breads with soy "milk" aren't turning out well, try boiling the liquid first then letting it cool before adding it to the rest of the ingredients. There may have been some bacteria that were meddling with the yeast and keeping it from doing its job.

· To replace nonfat dry milk powder in recipes, Ener-G Soy Quick, a powdered soy drink, worked beautifully in our test loaves. We saw other similar products in the health food stores such as: Fearn Soya Powder, Vitamite, and Better Than Milk. Ener-G's Nut Quick, an almond-based powdered beverage, caught our eye and is definitely on our long list of products to try in the future.

· As we've mentioned a few times, there's a product in the health food stores, also produced by Ener-G, called Egg Replacer. It's strictly a nondairy, nonanimal product made from ingredients such as potato starch, tapioca flour, and leavening. We've been very pleased with the results when substituting 2 teaspoons Egg Replacer plus 3 tablespoons water for each large egg in bread recipes. It even made a great "Egg" Bread!

· If you prefer not to use any commercially packaged egg replacement, you may simply omit the egg and replace it with a scant ¼ cup liquid.

· If you've already read through the long list of sugar substitutes in previous sections, you know that there are many ways to replace honey in bread recipes; probably the most closely related product is barley malt syrup. If you prefer not to use sugar at all, try diastatic malt powder. Replacing each tablespoon of sugar with ½ teaspoon malt powder produces good results.

WHEAT-FREE/GLUTEN-FREE BREADS

Until just a few years ago, if someone had asked us if it was possible to bake breads with 100 percent non-wheat and gluten-free flours, we would have replied, "No way!" Vital wheat gluten is just that: vital! We were very pleasantly surprised to discover a small group of people on the Prodigy network who were doing "the impossible." They were and are baking breads all the time without that crucial ingredient. Most of them have, or bake for people who have, an intolerance for any foods containing wheat and/or gluten. If a bread contains even the smallest amount of wheat, rye, oats, barley, millet, buckwheat, or triticale, it's unacceptable. Consequently, baking an edible bread becomes a real challenge. Add to that the rigidly programmed cycles of most bread machines, and producing an acceptable loaf of gluten-free bread is an incredible feat!

Fortunately, more and more sources for gluten-free recipes are showing up all the time, now that the bread machine has become so popular. We'd like to share some of the tried-and-true recipes and suggestions from a unique group of men and women on Prodigy. They were among the first to prove that it's possible to have fresher, better-tasting breads at a fraction of the cost health food stores charge.

· Xanthan gum is the "glue" that binds the bread dough together and replaces the gluten in these breads. It is a powder derived from a laboratory-grown organism called *xanthomonas compestris*. Most 1½-pound loaves use about 3½ teaspoons xanthan gum.

· Take it from two who learned the hard way, if you spill xanthan gum on the floor or countertop, you're better off vacuuming it up or brushing it into the sink with a dry towel than trying to clean it up with a wet cloth or sponge. Once wet, it becomes very gooey and a major headache to remove.

· Two other "gluten replacers" are guar gum and methylcellulose (methocel). Ener-G Foods (see Sources, page 215) stocks all three.

· Gluten-free ingredients for breads include white rice flour (coarse), white rice flour (fine), brown rice flour, sweet rice flour, rice bran, rice starch, rice polish, tapioca flour, tapioca starch, potato flour, potato starch flour, soy flour, yellow corn flour, white corn flour, yellow cornmeal, white cornmeal, polenta meal, cornstarch, corn bran, and acorn flour. There are also several flours made from such legumes as peas, mung beans, lentils, and garbanzo beans. The options are quite amazing, and are available at most health food stores. Others are available from sources listed in the back of this book (see page 215). The rest can be hand-milled.

· In addition to the above flours, Ener-G sells packaged gluten-free bread machine mixes. Experiment a little by adding chopped, dried fruits or herbs and spices to them for variety.

· Observe your bread dough during the first kneading cycle. If the machine has difficulty mixing the dough thoroughly, use a spatula carefully to assist it once or twice.

· Gluten-free bread dough does not form a smooth ball as does wheat flour dough. It more closely resembles whipped potatoes and doesn't always mix up well in the bread machine unless you watch it and assist it occasionally with a rubber spatula. We had more success by reversing the normal order of adding ingredients. Start with the yeast and dry ingredients, add half the wet ingredients, then press Start. Allow the ingredients to mix for a minute or so, then gradually add the rest of the liquids.

· Beat eggs well before adding them to the rest of the ingredients.

· Bread machines with a dough pin seemed to do the best job of mixing gluten-free breads.

· Universal Foods (Red Star Yeast) has a special gluten-free hotline: 1-800 4-CELIAC.

79

· The Celiac Sprue Association/USA, Inc., is a national support organization that offers information and referral services. They have published a series of low-cost brochures on the gluten-free diet, gluten-free commercial foods, and related topics. They also offer a newsletter as part of their annual membership fee. For information, you can call them from 10 A.M. to noon and from 1 to 3 P.M. Central time at 1-402-558-0600, or write to them: CSA/USA, Inc., P.O. Box 31700, Omaha, NE 68131-0700.

Gene's Basic Rice Bread

Gene Hill, who lives in Davis, California, bakes this bread at least twice a week. He recommends trying it as a toasted cheese sandwich.

1 cup fresh gluten-free buttermilk	¼ cup sugar
¼ cup butter, melted	3½ teaspoons xanthan gum
1 teaspoon rice vinegar	3 eggs
1½ teaspoons salt	½ cup water (for Welbilt/DAK and Zojirushi machines, add 2 tablespoons more water)
2 cups brown rice flour	
⅓ cup potato starch flour	1½ tablespoons active dry yeast
⅓ cup tapioca flour	

1. Place the buttermilk, melted butter, rice vinegar, and salt in bread pan. Stir with a rubber spatula.

2. In a large bowl, combine all the dry ingredients except the yeast. Mix well with a whisk.

3. In a separate bowl, combine the eggs and water; beat lightly.

4. Place ½ of the dry ingredients in the bread pan. Add the egg mixture. Add the remainder of the dry ingredients; sprinkle the yeast on top. Select Light Crust setting and press Start.

5. Observe the dough frequently during the kneading cycles. If it does not appear to be mixing well, use a rubber spatula to assist it occasionally.

6. After the baking cycle ends, remove bread from pan, place on wire rack, and allow to cool 1 hour before slicing.

VARIATIONS:

· You can substitute olive oil for the butter.

· Replace ¼ to ½ cup of the rice flour with another gluten-free flour, such as yellow or blue corn flour, polenta meal, or soy flour.

· You can add at least ¼ cup grated Cheddar cheese for a new flavor.

· Sauté some onions in the melted butter, allow them to cool, then add them and your favorite herbs to create an onion/herb bread.

CRUST: Light
OPTIONAL BAKE CYCLE: Sweet Bread/Rapid Bake

Bob's Cheddar Cheese Bread

*T*his rich bread is flecked with grated cheese. If you're daring, try adding 2 or 3 tablespoons of diced jalapeño peppers to it. It's also good toasted. We have Bob and Melody Gabriel to thank for sharing this gluten-free recipe.

1½-POUND LOAF	1-POUND LOAF
2¼ teaspoons (1 packet) active dry yeast	2 teaspoons active dry yeast
1 cup brown rice flour	1 cup brown rice flour
2 cups white rice flour	1½ cups white rice flour
3½ teaspoons xanthan gum	2 teaspoons xanthan gum
2 tablespoons sugar	1½ tablespoons sugar
1 teaspoon salt	¾ teaspoon salt
1½ cups (6 ounces) grated extra-sharp Cheddar cheese	1¼ cups (5 ounces) grated extra-sharp Cheddar cheese
¼ cup nonfat dry milk powder	3 tablespoons nonfat dry milk powder
2 tablespoons butter or margarine, softened	1¾ tablespoons butter or margarine, softened
2 large eggs, well beaten	1 extra large or jumbo egg, well beaten
1¾ cups warm water	1⅓ cups warm water

I. Place all ingredients, except the warm water, in bread pan, select Light Crust setting, and press Start. While the machine is kneading, gradually pour in the water. If the dough does not mix well, use a rubber spatula to assist it occasionally.

2. After the baking cycle ends, remove bread from pan, place on wire rack, and allow to cool 1 hour before slicing.

CRUST: Light
OPTIONAL BAKE CYCLES: Sweet Bread/Rapid Bake

Melody's Brown and White Bread

M elody Gabriel from Vero Beach, Florida, shared this basic, easy-to-make recipe and when others tried it, the consensus was "Wonderful!"

1½-POUND LOAF	1-POUND LOAF
2¼ teaspoons (1 packet) active dry yeast	2 teaspoons active dry yeast
1 cup brown rice flour	1 cup brown rice flour
2 cups white rice flour	1½ cups white rice flour
3½ teaspoons xanthan gum	2¾ teaspoons xanthan gum
¼ cup plus 2 teaspoons sugar	2 tablespoons sugar
1½ teaspoons salt	1 teaspoon salt
1⅓ cups nonfat dry milk powder	1 cup nonfat dry milk powder
¼ cup butter or margarine, melted	1 tablespoon butter or margarine, melted
2 large eggs, well beaten	1 extra large or jumbo egg, well beaten
1¾ cups warm water	1⅓ cups warm water

1. Place all ingredients, except the warm water, in bread pan and press Start. While the machine is kneading, gradually pour in the water. If the dough does not mix well, use a rubber spatula to assist it occasionally.

2. After the baking cycle ends, remove bread from pan, place on wire rack, and allow to cool 1 hour before slicing.

CRUST: Medium
OPTIONAL BAKE CYCLES: Sweet Bread/Rapid Bake

5
Helpful Hints and Troubleshooting Techniques

Tips for Baking the Perfect Loaf

Prior to Baking

· Within a week, most new owners realize that their bread machine is one of those rarities . . . a kitchen appliance that will remain on the countertop and be used constantly; it will not be relegated to some back corner of the pantry. If you can manage it, you will save time by storing all your bread-baking items in one area. We find it convenient to have small containers and jars of flour, sugar, brown sugar, nonfat dry milk, oats, oil, honey, molasses, salt, raisins, potato flakes, cornmeal, herbs, spices, and measuring utensils all within an arm's reach.

· Store your whole-grain flours, wheat germ, bran, nuts, and seeds (including sesame and poppy seeds) in the refrigerator or freezer. It's helpful to have a second freezer.

Baking Great Bread

· For the best breads, use the freshest ingredients.

· If your well-used bread pan seems to have lost its nonstick ability, spraying it lightly with a nonstick cooking spray before adding ingredients will ease the process of removing the baked bread later on.

· Learn to judge the dough as we discussed in the Essential Guidelines for Bread Machine Baking (page 13). It's a small step you can take when making a bread for the first time that will often prevent disappointing results four hours later.

· Use large eggs unless the recipe states otherwise.

· Use room-temperature ingredients for best results unless your instruction booklet says otherwise. Liquids should be heated to 80°F.

· Use a dry measuring cup to measure the dry ingredients and a glass or plastic liquid measuring cup to measure the liquids.

· Do not scoop up your flour with the measuring cup and then pack it in and level it off. That is the most common cause of dense, small loaves. With that method, you will add 1 to 2 tablespoons more flour *with each cup* to the recipe. Is it any wonder the dough is stiff and the gluten cannot form properly? Instead, gently spoon the flour from your canister into a dry measuring cup and then level it with a straight-edged knife or spatula.

· Avoid answering or talking on the phone while trying to measure ingredients for your next bread. We've ruined many loaves that way!

· We find it helpful to collect all the ingredients on the counter before adding them one by one to the bread pan; there seems to be less chance of omitting one of them. Yeast bread made without yeast is a monstrosity even the family pet will snub.

· Follow your manufacturer's directions as to the order in which you place the ingredients into the bread pan. However, unless your machine has a yeast dispenser that separates the yeast from the liquid ingredients, when using the Delayed-Bake timer we recommend adding the liquids first and the yeast last. Making a well in the dry ingredients for the yeast prevents it from coming in contact with the liquids too soon.

· The more ingredients you add to your dough, the heavier it will be. If it's a reluctant riser, you will have to either reduce the amount of additions or give the dough a boost with an enhancer such as extra gluten, ascorbic acid, or a commercial dough enhancer.

· Exceeding ¼, ⅓, or ½ cup of fat and/or sugar in 1-, 1½-, and 2-pound loaves respectively, will seriously impair the gluten's ability to develop properly.

· When using butter straight from the refrigerator, cut it into small pieces or soften it first in the microwave.

· Any time you add more than 2 tablespoons of butter or margarine to a recipe, cut the shortening into smaller pieces first.

· Whole-grain breads will not rise as high as breads made with all-white bread flour.

· If you want to use ingredients, such as Grape Nuts or granola, that have the potential to scratch the coated surface of your bread pan, add them with the liquids and let them soak several minutes to soften.

· Gluten absorbs water, so the higher the gluten level in your flour, the more liquid you will need to produce a soft, silky dough.

· Select the Light Crust setting when baking breads that are high in fat or sugar, or contain cheese, eggs, or whole-grain flours.

· When cooking or roasting any ingredients, be sure to let them cool to room temperature before adding them to the rest of the ingredients.

· To get the last little bit of honey or molasses out of the jar, warm it for 5 to 10 seconds in the microwave.

· It pays to peek at the dough near the end of its rising period. If it is threatening to overflow the pan, simply deflate it slightly by poking it once or twice with a toothpick.

Using the Dough Cycle; Baking Breads in the Oven

· If you prefer to make a bread on the dough cycle then bake it in the oven, turn it out onto a floured or lightly oiled countertop, shape it into a loaf or loaves, and place it in a greased 8½x4½-inch pan (for the 1-pound dough) or a 9x5-inch loaf pan (for the 1½-pound dough) or two 8½x4½-inch pans (for the 2-pound dough).

· To create a warm environment for rising doughs that you plan to bake outside the machine, turn on your oven to the lowest-setting (Warm) for one minute, then turn it off, and place the covered dough in the warm oven to rise.

· Do not cover rising doughs with terrycloth towels. They become imbedded in the dough.

· When baking breads in the oven instead of the bread machine, darker pans will produce darker crusts. If you choose a glass loaf pan, reduce the oven temperature by 25°F.

The Raisin/Nut Cycle

· When the machine beeps to add extras such as raisins, nuts, or dried fruits, avoid tossing the raisins and dried fruits into the bread pan all clumped together. They may not separate properly by the time the kneading cycle ends.

· Dusting the raisins and dried fruits with a little flour or cinnamon first will help them separate and mix into the dough.

· If you want a different flavor, while the dough is mixing, soak your raisins in some inexpensive vanilla, brandy, or rum. When the machine beeps to add extra ingredients, drain them well, then add.

· If you have no raisin/nut cycle or don't want to use it, try refrigerating or freezing your raisins, chopped dried fruits, and nuts. They hold their shape better and don't break down quite as easily. If you choose to freeze them, spread them out on a cookie sheet and place the sheet in the freezer. Once the separate pieces are frozen, you can place them in a heavy-duty plastic bag or container for longer storage.

· If your machine does not have a raisin/nut cycle and the ingredients added at the start are pulverized by the end of the second kneading cycle, you can set a timer to coincide with the last 10 minutes of your second kneading cycle. If you find that they're not being fully incorporated into the dough, then try adding them at the beginning of the second kneading cycle.

   · If you constantly miss the signal to add ingredients because your machine has a very soft "beep" or because you're not in the kitchen at the time, set a louder timer or carry one with you. Some gourmet kitchen stores and mail-order catalogs sell a small timer that you can wear like a necklace. This would be ideal. It's also a handy way of reminding yourself to check the dough every so often when trying a new recipe, if you tend to get busy with other projects.

AFTER THE BREAD IS BAKED

   · If you have difficulty removing a bread from the pan, rap the corner of the bread pan on a wooden cutting board or padded surface several times. Avoid sticking a knife or metal spatula into the pan to release it; you'll scratch the coating.

   · A good serrated bread knife is invaluable. If you're not pleased with your slicing skills, we've found that an electric knife helps produce more uniform slices. And if all else fails, there are some very compact electric food slicers that will produce perfect slices every time! You'll find them in kitchen specialty stores and catalogs.

   · We know . . . it's oh, so tempting to cut into that freshly baked loaf of bread the moment you turn it out of the bread pan. Try to wait at least 15 minutes to give it a chance to set up enough to be sliceable. A hot loaf of bread will collapse or compress if you try to slice it too soon.

   · Some breads bake up much softer than others. If you can, wait until the next day to slice those softies.

   · Get in the habit of keeping all the little pieces and parts of your bread pan together. A mixing blade lost down the disposal can mean *weeks* without homemade bread (and probably without a disposal)! If you know yourself well and see this one coming, you'd be wise to order a spare or two right now while you're thinking about it.

S.O.S.

   · We'd be remiss if we didn't mention our favorite source of friendly assistance, new ideas, and consumer feedback. Thousands of Web sites and newsgroups on the Internet offer bread recipes and information. Come visit ours at www.bread machinemagic.com. We have several links to other bread sites to get you started. If you have questions or comments, click on the little mailbox at the bottom and drop us an e-mail any time. There's also a very reputable online newsletter called *The Bread Digest* that we recommend. See our Sources section (page 215) for information on how to subscribe.

How to Adapt Your Favorite Recipes
for the Bread Machine

Once you're familiar with your machine and glowing with confidence because of all the "masterpieces" you've baked up, you'll probably want to branch out creatively. Wonderful childhood memories will slowly trickle back into your consciousness: Aunt Loretta's famous yeast rolls that you could never get enough of, the dark pungent breads your grandmother learned to bake in "the old country," or the incomparable Jewish rye breads from the corner deli. With the original recipe in hand or a reasonable facsimile you've found in a cookbook, you can duplicate those treasures. Here are some guidelines:

· First, you will have to reduce the volume of your original recipe to fit the flour and liquid capacities of your bread machine. You'll find that most recipes will have to be reduced by half or two-thirds to suit your machine.

· Once you reduce your recipe, the quantities of the essential ingredients should fall within the following parameters. Make minor adjustments if necessary.

1-POUND LOAF	1½-POUND LOAF	2-POUND LOAF
⅞ to 1 cup liquid	1⅛ to 1¼ cups liquid	1⅜ to 1½ cups liquid
¼ to 1 teaspoon salt	½ to 1½ teaspoons salt	¾ to 2 teaspoons salt
2 teaspoons to 3 tablespoons fat	1 to 5 tablespoons fat	2 to 7 tablespoons fat
2 teaspoons to 3 tablespoons sweetener	1 to 5 tablespoons sweetener	2 to 7 tablespoons sweetener
2 to 2½ cups flour*	3 to 3½ cups flour*	4 to 4½ cups flour*
1½ to 2½ teaspoons active dry yeast	1½ to 2½ teaspoons active dry yeast	2 to 3 teaspoons active dry yeast

*Whole-grain breads often require the larger amounts of flour to produce an acceptable-size loaf. You will probably have to increase the amount of liquid as well when using the extra flour.

· If your recipe reductions result in odd measurements such as ⅓ teaspoon cinnamon, you have a few options: You can approximate a ⅓ teaspoon measure by using a heaping ¼ teaspoon of the ingredient, or you can choose to add ¼ teaspoon or ½ teaspoon of the spice, according to your taste. Don't worry too much about fractional amounts of seasonings, etc.; it's the liquid, flour, and salt that are the crucial ingredients. Care should be taken to measure them accurately.

· One large egg equals a scant ¼ cup (4 tablespoons) liquid. If the original recipe, which you reduced by half, listed one egg, you can use either 2 tablespoons of liquid egg substitute to equal that ½ egg or add the entire egg but reduce the liquid in the recipe by the extra 2 tablespoons liquid in the whole egg.

· A word of advice: We've found ratios of 2:1, 2½:1, and 3:1 cups of wheat flour to cups of non-wheat flour work best in our bread machines. If your recipe is 100 percent whole grain with little or no wheat flour, you will need to adjust the proportions to include a minimum of 2 cups wheat flour for each cup of non-wheat flour to avoid creating a loaf that would break your foot if you dropped it.

· If you're re-creating a roll recipe or a specialty-type bread using the dough cycle, the dough is usually easier to handle if you reduce the liquid by 2 tablespoons. However, if this is too stiff a dough for your machine and it sounds like it's struggling to mix it, return the 2 tablespoons of liquid to the dough.

· When adapting a recipe for use in the bread machine, you should monitor it closely the first time you bake it. Jot down any adjustments you make to the dough during the kneading cycle. Observe the dough as it rises. If it rises too tall that first time, you'll know to reduce the liquid, yeast, or sugar or increase the amount of salt in the future.

· If, after several attempts to duplicate a favorite recipe, you end up with a great-tasting bread that refuses to bake up properly in the machine, don't give up on it. In the future, make it on the dough cycle, remove it from the machine, shape it, allow it to rise until doubled, then bake it in the oven!

· Yes, it is possible to do the reverse and convert a bread machine recipe into a traditional bake-by-hand recipe. Use these steps as a guideline: In a large bowl, dissolve active dry yeast in ½ cup warm water (105° to 115°F). (If you are using a quick rising or instant yeast, skip the first step.) Stir in the rest of the liquids (minus ¼ cup), salt, fat, sweetener, and all but 2 cups of the flour. With a mixer, beat until smooth. Stir in enough remaining flour to make the dough easy to handle. Turn out onto a lightly floured surface. Knead until smooth and elastic, about 15 minutes. Dust counter with additional flour if dough becomes too sticky to handle while kneading. Place in an oiled bowl, turn oiled side up, cover, and let rise in a warm location until doubled in size, about 1½ hours. If you stick a finger into the center of the dough and the impression remains, the dough is ready. Punch down dough. Divide 2-pound dough in half. (Bread can be baked freeform on a greased baking sheet or shaped and placed into a greased loaf pan(s). Use an 8½x4½-inch pan for the 1-pound dough, a 9x5-inch loaf pan for the 1½-pound dough, and two 8½x4½-inch pans for the 2-pound dough.) Cover and let rise again until doubled, 30 to 60 minutes. Bake most breads at 375°F for approximately 35 to 45 minutes. Bake breads high in fat or sugar at 350°F for approximately 35 to 45 minutes. Bake breads with little or no fat or sugar (such as French breads) at 400°F to 450°F for 20 to 40 minutes.

THE NEXT STEP:
HOW TO CREATE YOUR OWN RECIPES

If you've adapted several of your favorite recipes successfully, the next step is to try your hand at creating a few of your own. With the following guidelines, you should be able to develop a one-of-a-kind masterpiece that will make you proud!

· For a starting point, refer to the generic 1-, 1½-, and 2-pound recipes on page 90.

· Use a minimum of ⅜ cup of liquid for each cup of flour. We found it easier to start with a dry dough and add liquid when necessary during the kneading cycle than to try and correct an overly wet dough.

· If you choose to include "wet" ingredients such as sour cream, cottage cheese, yogurt, mashed potatoes, fruits, and vegetables, you must consider them as part of your liquids. As a general rule of thumb, regard them as half liquid and deduct that amount of liquid from your basic recipe. Adding ½ cup of chopped onions means reducing the liquid in your recipe by ¼ cup. Watch the bread dough while it is kneading. If it looks too wet or too dry, add flour or water as needed, 1 tablespoon at a time

· When using eggs in your recipe, calculate each large egg as the equivalent of a scant ¼ cup of liquid.

· Keep in mind that the more you add beyond the basics of flour, liquid, sugar, salt, fat, and yeast, the heavier the bread will be and the longer it will take to rise. Limit them to roughly ¼ of your total flour; i.e., ½ cup of extras for 2 cups of flour, ¾ cup of extras for 3 cups of flour, 1 cup of extras for 4 cups of flour. Extras include items such as: dried fruits, nuts, seeds, whole grains, and raisins.

· We found ratios of 2:1, 2½:1, and 3:1 cups of wheat flour to cups of non-wheat flour to work best in our bread machines. For instance, if you want to create a rye bread, experiment using 1 cup of rye flour and 2, 2½, or 3 cups of wheat flour (that can be a mixture of white and whole wheat). For the smaller 1-pound machine a 3:1 ratio would mean ½ cup rye flour and 1½ cups wheat flour.

· Start with ½ teaspoon of salt per cup of flour; in some cases you will be able to reduce that amount, even by as much as half. But don't try to omit it altogether. Salt is critical to the success of the bread.

· Most loaves don't need more than ½ tablespoon fat per cup of flour.

· The average amount of sugar per cup of flour is ½ tablespoon.

· Do not add more than 2 tablespoons butter or sugar per cup of flour to any loaf.

· Yeast amounts vary according to brand and type. Most loaves need a minimum of 1½ teaspoons active dry yeast. Use ½ teaspoon instant or fast-rising yeast per cup of flour if you plan to bake the loaf on the Regular cycle and double that amount if you plan to bake it on the Rapid Bake cycle.

· Watch the dough closely during both kneading cycles. After several minutes of kneading, if it looks too dry or wet or feels stiff when pinched, make the proper adjustments. By the end of the second kneading cycle, it should form a smooth, pliable ball of dough.

· It pays to observe and take notes each time you attempt a new bread.

· When you make corrections to a recipe, try to limit them to one change at a time. Often times simply adjusting the amount of liquid will make all the difference you really need. If you increase the yeast, decrease the salt, and increase the sugar at the same time, you'll never know which change was the effective one.

· Don't get too discouraged if your first efforts aren't stellar successes. Most "blue-ribbon" breads take several attempts before perfection is achieved.

· By all means, let your creative juices flow! Once you start concocting your own bread recipes, trips to the grocery and health food store can be an adventure. Have fun . . . pick something new each time to incorporate into your next creation.

HOME MILLING

If you want to take homemade, healthy bread baking to new heights, the next step is to purchase a manual or electric grain mill. Once you try breads made from grains you grind into flour yourself, you may never return to commercially milled whole-grain flours! Freshly milled wheat is much sweeter than store-bought whole wheat flour, which can often have a bitter undertaste. We recommend using freshly milled wheat in a very simple, low-sugar recipe to capture its naturally sweet essence and delicate richness.

Freshly ground whole-grains will turn rancid rather quickly so grind up only what you plan to use. (The whole-grain kernels will keep at room temperature indefinitely.) We've found that 1 cup of wheat berries produces a scant 1¾ cups flour. One pound of wheat berries equals approximately 4½ cups flour. We wish we could also tell you the calories burnt per minute when you grind it manually but so far we haven't seen that listed on any exercise chart! It should be; it's a bit of a workout. We think it's comparable to chopping your own wood for the evening fire . . . the fire burns just that much warmer; the bread tastes just that much sweeter.

We've listed several sources (see page 215) for mills and whole grains. When you're in the market for a grain mill, ask questions based on your intended usage and look for one that is easy to take apart and thoroughly clean. We also found that we could purchase 50-pound sacks of hard, red, winter wheat berries from local health food stores. Ask the manager. They may be willing to discount the price, too.

Depending on your type of mill, there's a wide variety of grains, beans, seeds, and nuts you can grind into flour for your breads: wheat, rye, corn, rice, barley, oats, buckwheat, millet, kamut, quinoa, peas, mung beans, garbanzos, and lentils for starters. We've even heard of acorn flour, but you might have to fight the little chipmunks and squirrels for them. Let loose your imagination . . . just think of all the delicious, new breads you can concoct. So come on . . . let's get cranking!

HOW TO COUNTERACT TROUBLESOME CLIMATIC CONDITIONS

There's no getting around it . . . the weather has a definite effect on your bread. When you bake a particular loaf day after day with varying results, changes in the weather are often the cause. When it's humid, the flour will be more moist than usual and won't absorb as much of the liquids you add. If you use the amount of liquid the recipe calls for, your doughs will often be too wet and bake up with a coarse, holey texture. Conversely, when it is extremely dry outside, your flour will be very "thirsty" and, without adjustments, the baked bread will be heavy and dry. Here's what you can do to work with Mother Nature:

· On humid days, decrease the liquid in the recipe by 2 tablespoons. Watch the dough as it mixes. If you think it needs just a little more moisture, add liquid a teaspoon at a time. As it nears the end of the second kneading cycle, it should be a smooth, pliable, slightly tacky ball of dough.

· When the weather is dry, observe your dough during the kneading cycle. If you think it looks dry, add extra liquid a teaspoon at a time until it forms that silky smooth ball.

· Some people who live in very humid or dry climates find it more accurate to weigh rather than measure the flour. If you choose to do so, the helpful people at General Mills (Gold Medal flour) informed us that 1 cup all-purpose flour weighs 4.59 ounces (130 grams), 1 cup bread flour weighs 4.76 ounces (135 grams), and 1 cup whole wheat flour weighs 4.51 ounces (128 grams).

· During the cold winter months, extra care has to be taken to keep your machine away from cold exterior walls, chilly windows, and cold drafts. It's time to move the bread machine out of the cold laundry room or garage into a warmer room in the house. If you normally don't warm your liquids during the rest of the year, you may have to do so on exceptionally cold days.

· Summer means heat and that can bring its own problems. Doughs tend to rise faster and higher when it's warm in the house. It can mean that normally tall breads will suddenly overflow the pan or collapse during baking. To cool the dough, start with refrigerated ingredients and cold liquids or choose a cooler time of day to bake. Also, during those hot summer days, keep the bread machine out of drafts caused by air-conditioning or ceiling fans.

ADJUSTMENTS FOR HIGH-ALTITUDE BREAD BAKING

If you're a bread machine owner and live 3,000 feet or more above sea level, you may be experiencing some sunken loaves. At higher elevations, the dough "overproofs." Due to the lower barometric pressure at high altitudes, the carbon dioxide gas bubbles created by the yeast expand more rapidly. Therefore, the bread rises too high, the gluten loses its strength, and the bread collapses during baking. Take heart, it's an easy problem to correct. No need to pack up your bread machine and move down to the flatlands. Try the following combination of suggestions:

· Reduce the amount of yeast by about 1/3. This will create less carbon dioxide and the bread will not rise as quickly.

· Increase the salt by 25 percent. This will have the same effect as decreasing the yeast. The bread will rise slower and be less likely to sink during baking.

· Add from 1/2 to 1 tablespoon gluten per cup of flour. Increasing the gluten will give added strength to your bread.

· Watch your dough as it mixes. You may need to add at least 1 to 3 tablespoons more liquid since flour stored at high altitudes tend to be drier than that stored below 3,000 feet.

(These recommended alterations were shared by Irwin Franzel, a friend and very knowledgeable bread machine baker. With his "Zoji" S-15 under one arm and bread-baking supplies under the other, he took off for a Colorado vacation and baked up numerous loaves of "high-altitude" bread. By adjusting the salt, gluten, yeast, and liquid, he was finally able to produce consistently well-shaped bread.)

· Two other options: Because of the rapid-rising nature of high-altitude breads, try baking them on the Rapid Bake cycle of your machine to reduce the rising time. If your machine has a programmable mode, watch the loaf as it rises; when it nears the top of the bread pan, switch to the Bake cycle manually.

SMALL LOAVES: A MULTITUDE OF CAUSES AND THE SOLUTIONS

We've observed that the most common problem faced by bread machine owners is bread that fails to rise properly. As you can see from the following list, there are any number of reasons why that happens as frequently as it does. We've started with the most common causes and listed the rest in an approximate order of their occurrence.

By the way, if you're only having problems with a bread not rising properly, we suggest you make only one change at a time when you're trying to correct the problem. That way, you'll be able to clearly identify the correction(s) that works.

· *Were you baking a 100 percent whole wheat bread?*
Whole wheat breads will normally not rise as high as white flour breads. The bran and wheat germ they contain make the flour heavier than white flour. To give it a boost, add 1 tablespoon gluten per cup of flour or replace part of the whole wheat flour with white bread flour.

· *Were you baking a whole-grain bread that had a very low proportion of wheat flour to non-wheat flour?*
In all the breads we've tasted, the best results were achieved by using a minimum of 2 cups wheat flour for every cup of non-wheat flour.

· *Was the bread dough dry and very stiff as it was kneading?*
Next time, as it kneads, add more liquid 1 tablespoon at a time until the dough forms a silky-smooth, pliable ball of dough.

· *Were there too many "heavy" extras such as raisins, bran, whole grains, seeds, or nuts?*
The more you add to the basic dough, the more it will weigh it down and make it harder to rise. Limit those extras to ¼ cup per cup of flour.

· Did you use a stone-ground or coarse hand-milled whole-grain flour?

The gluten in coarse-textured flour does not develop as well as the gluten in finely milled flours. You may have to use a dough enhancer to increase the height of your next loaves.

· Is your tap water very hard?

To counteract it and create a more yeast-friendly acidic environment, add 1 teaspoon lemon juice or vinegar to the water.

· Did you use all-purpose flour rather than bread flour?

The difference in gluten content between the two flours can make a significant difference in the height of your bread.

· Did you bake the bread on a Rapid Bake cycle?

Many times our test loaves baked on the Rapid Bake cycle were up to one inch smaller than those baked on the Regular cycle. In addition, not all loaves bake up well on the faster cycle, especially those that are high in fat or laden with extras.

· Has your yeast lost its vitality?

Refer to page 40 for directions on how to test your yeast's activity.

· What brand of yeast did you use?

We've found that different brands of yeast vary in their effectiveness in the bread machine. We recommend Red Star yeast.

· Are you a "flour scooper?"

Scooping the flour out of the bag or canister will result in adding much more flour to the dough than the recipe calls for. Measure the flour by lightly spooning it into the measuring cup then leveling it off.

· Were most of your ingredients taken from the refrigerator or freezer?

Doughs created with room-temperature ingredients produce the best breads. Try to plan ahead and remove ingredients from the fridge or freezer at least ½ hour in advance. If this isn't possible, set your bread on a Delayed-Bake timer and allow it to sit at room temperature for at least ½ hour before starting.

· *If your machine has a Preheat cycle, did you place the bread pan in the machine and press Start immediately?*

If you have a machine with a Preheat cycle that warms the ingredients before mixing, you should wait at least 30 seconds before pressing Start to give the sensor time to register the cold ingredients. Also, keep the sensor and the bottom of the pan clean and lint free.

· *Were your liquids too hot?*

Start with liquids at 80°F (approximately room temperature). If they're too hot, they will kill the yeast.

· *Were your liquids too cold?*

If you used liquids straight from the refrigerator and your machine doesn't have a Preheat cycle, they were too cold for the yeast to activate properly.

· *Did you add more salt or salty ingredients to the recipe?*

Salt inhibits the yeast's growth. If you want to add salty ingredients, reduce the salt amount listed in the recipe.

· *Did you omit the sugar accidentally or on purpose?*

We've been able to bake some breads without sugar or any of its substitutes but not 100 percent of the time. The sweetener is usually an essential ingredient. If you choose to bake breads without it, try Sweet One, Sugar Twin, or diastatic malt powder.

· *Did you use an excessive amount of dark brown or golden spices?*

Spices such as cinnamon, nutmeg, cloves, cardamom, mace, allspice, ginger, and mustard contain compounds which are toxic to yeast. Limit their amount to a scant ½ teaspoon per cup of flour.

· *Did you forget to add the yeast?*

If this was the cause of your small loaf, you'll know it . . . it just never rose. Place all your ingredients out on the counter before you begin measuring from now on.

· *Did you dump the yeast into the bread pan right on top of the salt?*

Salt and yeast don't mix. A high concentration of salt can kill the yeast if they come in contact with one another.

· *Did you forget to install the mixing blade?*

It's amazing how often this happens! Get in the habit of checking the dough as it begins to mix and you'll catch this in time to correct it. (Sticking your hand into that goop and blindly fumbling around to line up the post and the blade correctly will be an experience you won't soon forget!)

· *Are you experiencing an extreme weather condition: is it either very humid or incredibly dry?*

If it's very humid, start by decreasing the liquid in the recipe by 2 tablespoons; adjust as needed while the dough is mixing. If the air is very dry, you may have to add liquid as the dough is kneading.

· *Do you find in the wintertime that your breads are smaller?*

When it's cold, move your bread machine to a warm location. Avoid putting it near cold exterior walls, chilly windows, or in a draft. Turn up the heater if your home is especially chilly.

· *Did the mixing blade fail to function properly?*

Make sure it's pushed all the way down onto the post before you begin adding ingredients.

· *Did the dough fail to mix well?*

Make sure the bread pan is seated correctly in the machine; push it in until it clicks into place. (Or, in some machines, rotate it until you feel it lock into place and it won't lift out.)

· *Is your machine not kneading the dough as well as it used to; consequently, the gluten isn't being fully developed?*

It's possible the belt is stretched or slipping. Take your bread machine to a dependable appliance repair store that can replace the belt for you.

· *Was there any soap residue left in the bread pan after washing?*

Traces of soap will interfere with the yeast. Make sure you rinse your bread pan well after washing it.

· *Were you interrupted by a phone call in the middle of measuring your ingredients?*

It's possible you omitted or mismeasured something. Try again. Send the "dud" to the person who called (just kidding).

· *Do you have a lively curiosity and no window in the lid of your bread machine?*

If you open the lid of the machine often, especially during the rising phase, you release the warm air the dough needs to rise properly.

· *Was the recipe high in fat or high in sugar?*

Limit the amount of each to ¼ cup (1-pound loaf) or ⅓ cup (1½-pound loaf).

· *Was your flour old and stale?*

Flour sold in the markets has a shelf life of 15 months but if it was stored improperly at home or allowed to get too hot or damp, it may have gone stale. Throw it out and buy a fresh bag.

· *Did you accidentally knock the machine or drop the lid during the rising phase?*

Sudden jolts can sometimes deflate a dough.

· *Did you use raw, unpasteurized honey?*

Heat it first (don't exceed 180°F).

· *Are you measuring your liquids by tablespoons rather than in a measuring cup?*

For the most accurate liquid measurement, use the measuring cup that came with your machine or a liquid measuring cup. Place it on a level surface and judge the amount at eye level.

· *In the unlikely event you answered "no" to all the preceding questions, here are a few more bread-raising tips:*

Increase the amount of yeast and sugar slightly.

Replace a scant ¼ cup of the liquid with 1 egg for extra leavening.

Whole wheat breads can benefit from an extra kneading in most machines. After the first kneading cycle, stop the machine and restart it.

Try weighing your flour rather than measuring it. If you live in an area of the country that experiences extremes in weather conditions, weighing the flour will take the moisture content of the air and your flour into account. (See "Measurements" on page 17 for correct weights.)

Add lecithin (¼ teaspoon per cup of flour). It seems to work most effectively when combined with added gluten.

Keep in mind that a very tall loaf isn't always the ultimate objective. We've baked lid-thumpers that were all air and no body. Several of our favorite whole-grain breads are heavy, dense, and meant to be very thinly sliced.

Sunken Loaves: What Went Wrong

· *Was the dough quite wet during the kneading cycle?*

Reduce the liquid in the recipe next time you bake that bread or add flour as it is mixing, 1 tablespoon at a time, until the dough forms a satiny-smooth ball.

· *Did you use a fast-rising or instant yeast?*

The dough may have overproofed. Use ½ teaspoon fast-rising or instant yeast per cup of flour.

· *Did you omit or greatly reduce the amount of salt?*

The salt helps prevent the dough from overproofing. For the bread to rise properly, you need to add some salt. If you want to reduce the amount of sodium, substitute Morton Lite Salt for table salt.

· *Was the machine knocked or the lid dropped near the end of the rising phase?*

A sudden jolt can deflate a loaf.

· *Is the bread machine in a drafty location?*

A cold draft can cause a bread to sink.

· *Do you live at an altitude above 3,000 feet?*

Refer to page 95 for suggestions on how to alter your recipes for high-altitude baking.

LOAVES THAT HAVE MUSHROOM TOPS
OR OVERFLOW: HOW TO PREVENT THEM

· *Was the dough quite wet or did you add ingredients that increased the moisture content of the dough, such as fruits and vegetables?*

A too-wet dough can produce a variety of problems. In some cases, the bread will simply rise too high and overflow the pan; other times it will only threaten to overflow and produce a puffy, mushroomed top. An overly wet dough can also produce a bread that is very soft and spongy; when it's removed from the machine, the sides will collapse.

If you add extras that are moist, consider half their measure as liquid. Reduce the liquid in the recipe accordingly.

· *If the dough was very dry and crumbly while it was kneading, did you have to add more than 3 or 4 tablespoons of additional liquid to correct it?*

Next time, rather than adding so much more liquid, reduce the amount of flour instead.

· *Was the recipe too large for your machine?*

Recipes for 1-pound loaves consist of 2 cups of flour and approximately ⅞ cup of liquid. The 1½-pound recipe should have 3 cups flour and about 1¼ cups liquid. Recipes for 2-pound loaves will call for 4 cups flour and at least 1⅜ cups liquid. (In all cases, the amounts can be increased by approximately ⅓ for the smaller whole-grain breads.) Using quantities much in excess of these can result in breads that will rise too high for the bread pan.

· *Is your 2-pound bread pan too small?*

We have seen 2-pound bread pans that were no larger than the average 1½-pound bread pan. It's quite likely there will be overflows with these pans. If you now wonder if your bread pan is one of those, here's a simple test you can perform. If your vertical bread pan will hold 13 cups of water, it should be okay. Please note that the horizontal pans seem to be a little more forgiving. We didn't have the same overflow problems with them. In any case, if you have a 2-pound machine, we strongly suggest that you always start with the medium (1½-pound) recipes first. If a particular recipe is a very high riser, you'll know not to tempt the fates with the large version.

- *Did you omit or greatly reduce the amount of salt?*

Without salt, the yeast is uncontrolled and can produce a very tall loaf that will either collapse or overflow the pan.

- *Did the recipe call for a large amount of yeast?*

Reduce the yeast next time. As a guideline, figure about ½ teaspoon yeast per cup of flour. In some recipes, you may want to add an additional ½ teaspoon yeast to the total.

- *Was the recipe loaded with sweet ingredients?*

Try cutting back on the sugar in the future.

- *Did you use a fast-rising or instant yeast?*

This type of yeast can force a large loaf to rise too high, too quickly, and exceed the bounds of the bread pan.

- *Was it a hot day?*

You'll find that your loaves will rise very enthusiastically when the weather is warm. To slow them down a bit, use colder liquids or choose a cooler time of day to bake. You may have better results using the Rapid Bake cycle on those hot days.

- *Is this a favorite recipe that you're unwilling to alter, yet it consistently rises too high?*

Try baking it on the Rapid Bake cycle.

- *Did you go nuts with all those dough enhancers?*

If you threw in the works—gluten, lecithin, vinegar, ascorbic acid—were you all that surprised when it overflowed?

A FEW EXTRA TIPS

Just as it's a good habit to check the dough when it first begins mixing (ensuring that the mixing blade has been installed), it's also wise when you're home to peek at the bread near the end of the rising phase. If it is on the verge of overflowing the bread pan, you can prevent disaster by merely pricking the dough with a toothpick a few times to deflate it. It may not bake up picture perfect, but you'll save yourself a mammoth cleanup job. (We speak from experience).

If it's a new recipe, try to be home the first time you make it to check on its progress occasionally.

An Assortment of Common Problems: Their Causes and Cures

Raw, Doughy Spots in the Center or Top of the Loaf

· Too much heat escaped from the machine as the bread was baking.

· The recipe was too large for your machine.

· Too many rich or heavy ingredients and too short a Regular Bake cycle to bake the bread properly.

· If your bread machine has a glass dome, cover it with foil during the baking cycle. (Take care not to let the foil hang down and cover the air vents.)

· Use a smaller-size recipe next time.

· If your Regular Bake cycle is a Rapid Bake (3 hours or less), you may need to reduce the fat and/or added ingredients in certain recipes, such as raisin breads and holiday breads. They take too long to rise in Rapid Bake machines unless lightened up.

A Large Crack Around or on Top of the Loaf

· The dough was too dry.

· The dough may have been underproofed; it didn't rise long enough before the Bake cycle began.

· Next time add 1 to 2 tablespoons more liquid.

· If you have a bread machine with the programmable feature, increase the rising time for that particular loaf.

Is It a Loaf of Bread or a Doorstop?—The Loaf That Never Even Mixed; It Baked Up in Layers and Was Three Inches Tall

· This one's easy . . . someone forgot to put the mixing blade in before adding all the ingredients.

· A variation on that theme: You remember the mixing blade but didn't insert it far enough down on the post.

· Variation #2: The blade was correctly installed but the bread pan itself was not well seated in the machine, so the mixing blade didn't engage properly.

BURNT CRUSTS

· Set the crust color to Light.
· Choose the Sweet Bread setting, if your machine has it.
· Reduce the amount of sugar.
· Remove the loaf from the machine five or ten minutes before the Bake cycle ends.

PALE LOAVES

· Increase the sugar.
· Add fresh or instant milk to the dough.
· Set the crust color darker.

A LARGE AIR BUBBLE UNDER THE CRUST OR IN THE CENTER OF THE LOAF

· The dough was not well mixed or didn't deflate properly during the "punch down" between risings.
· It's normally a rare occurrence; if it continues to happen in a particular loaf, try adding 1 or 2 tablespoons more liquid next time.

CRUST TOO TOUGH AND CHEWY

· Increase the fat in the recipe.
· Add more milk, less water.
· Brush the crust lightly with melted butter when you remove it from the pan.
· As soon as the bread cools, place it in a plastic bag. Don't allow it to sit out for hours.
· If your machine has a Cool-Down cycle, leave the bread in the machine until the cooling cycle ends, rather than removing it immediately after the baking ends.

The Crust Was Too Soft; You Prefer It Crisp

- Reduce or eliminate the fat in your bread.
- Substitute water for milk in the recipe.
- Use the French Bread setting if your machine has it.
- As soon as the bread finishes baking, remove it from the bread pan.
- Do not place the bread in a plastic bag as soon as it cools.

The Crust Was Too Crisp; You Prefer It Soft

- Increase the fat in your bread.
- Use milk instead of water in the recipe.
- Do not use the French Bread setting.
- Allow the bread to cool in the machine, if it has a Cool-Down cycle.
- When the bread cools completely, place it in a sealed plastic bag.

Coarse, Holey-Textured Breads

- The dough was too wet or contained too many wet ingredients.
- The salt was omitted.
- You substituted applesauce (or other puréed fruits) for the butter in the recipe but didn't reduce the liquid by an equal measure.
- Decrease the liquids.
- When adding "wet" ingredients such as fruits and vegetables, consider half their measure as liquid and adjust the other liquids in the recipe accordingly.

Blisters on the Top of the Loaf

- The dough did not have a long enough rising time.
- If you have a machine with a programmable mode or a Whole Wheat cycle, use it to increase the rising time for that particular loaf.

Strong Yeasty Flavor

- Reduce the amount of yeast next time.

Soft-sided Loaves That Collapsed on One or All Sides

· The recipe had too much liquid.

· "Wet" ingredients were added to the dough and not taken into account.

· The bread was left in the pan after it finished baking and became very soggy.

· Reduce the liquid amount next time or add flour 1 tablespoon at a time during the kneading cycle.

· Remove the bread from the machine as soon as it is finished baking.

Dry Bread

· Eggs cause breads to be drier than usual.

· Dry grains such as oatmeal were added, which soaked up moisture from the bread dough.

· Breads low in fat and/or sugar dry out rapidly.

· The bread was left out too long to cool and dried out.

· The bread was stored in the refrigerator.

· Add extra oil or fat to counteract eggs' drying effect.

· When adding dry grains to breads, either soak them first or increase the liquid in the recipe.

· Increase fat and/or sugar in the recipe.

· Replace granulated sugar with honey. Replace fat with an equal amount of applesauce.

· Ingredients such as fat, honey, fruits, and oatmeal help bread retain its moisture longer.

· Once bread has cooled, place it in a plastic bag.

· Breads stored in the refrigerator will dry out and turn stale several times faster than bread stored at room temperature.

Coarse, Crumbly Texture

· The bread was too dry.

· It did not contain enough gluten.

· There may have been too many added cereals, grains, meals, and/or non-gluten flours.

· The salt was omitted.

· Dry, uncooked whole grains were added, which robbed the dough of its moisture.

· Reduce the amount of extra ingredients such as wheat bran, wheat germ, cornmeal, etc.

· Increase the liquid if the dough appears dry during kneading.

· When adding dry grains such as oats, multigrain cereal, or cornmeal, soak them first or increase the liquid in the recipe.

FUNKY, GNARLY SHAPED LOAVES

· This is a catchall category for any loaf that looks so weird, you're afraid to slice it open, much less offer samples to anyone you love.

· Sorry, you're on your own on this one!

· (If it's any consolation, even the "pros" goof up big time on occasion. You haven't lived until you've almost burnt down a store at a book signing because you forgot to add the liquid to that herb bread you intended to bake. Nothing like a little smoke and the foul smell of burnt flour to entice customers to buy your cookbook.)

REFRIGERATING/FREEZING BREAD DOUGH

REFRIGERATING DOUGH

· When the machine beeps, remove the dough from the pan and place it in a lightly oiled bowl with a tight-fitting lid or a large, oiled, plastic bag.

· You can store dough in the refrigerator for up to 5 days. Check it daily. It will rise very slowly and need punching down every day or so.

· When ready to use, remove the dough from the refrigerator 1½ to 2 hours before you plan to use it; this will bring it fully up to room temperature. (The time will vary according to the warmth of the room.) When the dough is room temperature, shape as desired, then place in a warm location to rise until doubled in size. Bake according to recipe directions.

· You can also remove the dough from the machine and shape it into dinner rolls, a loaf of bread, or a coffee cake. Cover and place the shaped dough in the coldest spot in the refrigerator. If made in the morning, you can bake it for dinner. Made at night, it will be ready for breakfast the next morning. Remove it from the refrigerator, let it come to room temperature, place in a warm location to rise until doubled in size, if necessary, then bake.

Freezing Dough

· Remove the dough from the bread pan, shape as desired, wrap it up well, and freeze.

· Dough can be frozen for up to one month.

· When you're ready to use the dough, remove it from the freezer the night before and allow it to thaw in the refrigerator overnight.

· If you want to defrost the dough at room temperature, allow 3 to 4 hours. Small rolls may take only 2 hours. If the dough is shaped into a loaf, it may take up to 6 hours, depending on the warmth of the room.

· Once thawed, place the dough in a warm location to rise. You'll find that the dough will take quite a bit longer to rise than usual. Bake as directed.

Here are just a few of the reasons to consider making a dough and then refrigerating or freezing it for later use:

· You can prepare a dough at your convenience and then bake it up fresh for a special meal. (We often do this with fat-free French bread dough because it goes stale so quickly if baked early in the day.)

· If the dough is prepared but something comes up, all is not lost. Just pop it into the refrigerator.

· It enables you to prepare dough in advance to take with you when you go camping for the weekend.

· You can prepare several batches of a dough in advance then bake them up all on the same day for a party or as gifts.

· You can duplicate a recipe that calls for dough or triple the amount of ingredients your machine can handle by making it in batches, then combining them and baking the loaf in the oven.

· Prepare a pizza dough in the morning or the night before. When you come home from work, you can throw together a fabulous homemade pizza in less time than it takes to have one delivered!

· Freeze shaped dinner rolls on a cookie sheet (once frozen transfer to a plastic bag) and you can bake up just the quantity you desire for dinner and not the entire batch.

· You can prepare cinnamon rolls the night before and place them in the refrigerator to rise slowly. The next morning bring them to room temperature and bake them for breakfast. No need to get up at 4 A.M.!

· Prepare an apple strudel in the morning, let it slowly rise in the refrigerator all day, and bake it up as you sit down for dinner that night. It's a wonderful dessert after a light meal.

· Prepare the dough for hamburger buns and bake them up as needed. If you don't use all of the dough within 5 days, you can freeze it in single portions or go ahead and bake up the remaining buns and freeze them in heavy plastic bags to have on hand.

· When your grandchildren come to visit for several days, have dough on hand so you can make teddy bears or pita bread with them when there's a lull in the activities.

Storing Bread

· To retain the crisp crust of French and sourdough breads, do not store them in plastic bags. Until sliced, you can leave them out as is. Once cut, place them in a large paper bag.

· When you remove the bread from the bread pan, place it on a rack to cool for at least 1 hour.

· Once fully cooled, place the loaf in a plastic bag, plastic container, or bread box. (Storage in plastic bags or containers will soften and change the bread's texture. You may prefer to store all your breads in paper; however, they will dry out and stale sooner than those stored in plastic.)

· If the bread is for immediate use, place it in a bag and leave it out at room temperature. Most breads will remain fresh for 2 to 3 days.

· To "freshen" and warm a several-day-old loaf for dinner, wrap it well in foil, heat at 300°F for 15 minutes until heated through.

· Breads made with honey, fruits, and fats will stay moist longer.

· Egg breads will dry out faster than usual. Adding extra oil to the bread will help counteract that.

· Do not store breads in the refrigerator. They will dry out and stale several times faster than when stored at room temperature.

· For longer storage, wrap the loaf well and place it in the freezer. It will keep up to 3 months there. To serve it warm at a meal, wrap the loaf in foil, place it in a 400°F oven for 10 minutes or so until heated through.

· Freezing destroys vitamin E.

· Though breads will not dry out as quickly if left whole when frozen, we prefer to slice the loaf once it cools and then place in plastic bags for freezing. That way, you can remove the number of slices desired from the bag without having to defrost the entire loaf for 1 or 2 slices.

· Thaw each slice in the microwave for about 15 seconds on HIGH.

CLEANING YOUR MACHINE

· We've heard of people cleaning the inside of their bread machine with everything from a portable hand vacuum to the tiny vacuums used to clean computer keyboards. Lois has even used an eyebrow brush and an old toothbrush. Hey, whatever works! A few times around with a damp dishcloth or paper towel does the job, too. What you shouldn't do is turn your machine upside down and vigorously shake it.

· If your machine has a sensor in the bottom that activates a Preheating cycle, keep it clean and free of lint.

· As soon as you remove the bread from the pan, fill the pan with warm, soapy water. Let it sit for at least 10 minutes. That will enable you to remove the mixing blade without a great deal of trouble. If you allow the dough to dry out inside the blade, it will be a struggle trying to remove it.

· If the blade is difficult to remove, even after soaking, hold it with one hand and, with the other, hold the knob opposite it on the bottom of the pan. There should be a little give; move the blade back and forth until you can work it loose.

· It's easier to remove the bread dough from the mixing shaft in the Welbilt/DAK machines if you do so while it is still warm and soft. Use a damp dishcloth. If the dough is allowed to cool and harden, you will have to resoften it by wrapping a damp dishcloth around the shaft for several minutes to facilitate cleaning.

· The most effective way to clean the inside of the mixing blade is with the small end of a baby-bottle brush. It fits perfectly inside the hole.

· Wash the inside of the pan well with soapy water and a soft cloth or sponge. Do not use anything abrasive that will destroy the nonstick coating.

· Rinse the pan and mixing blade thoroughly. Any soap residue can interfere with the next bread you bake, causing a small loaf.

· Once they are clean, place all the little bits and pieces (such as the mixing blade, the dough pin, and the rubber seal) inside the pan so they won't disappear and cause a family crisis.

OUR FAVORITE ACCESSORIES:
THE LITTLE EXTRAS THAT ADD TO
THE FUN OF BAKING HOMEMADE BREAD

If you've read the entire book up to this point, you deserve a break. It's time to go shopping! We thought we'd lighten it up a bit here and share the contents of our baking cabinets and gadget drawers. Over the years, the two of us have collected hundreds of "can't-live-without" kitchen tools and many of them are seeing new life as useful bread-baking accessories. Maybe one or two will strike your fancy, also. Here are some of our favorites:

· At the top of our list is a purchase that has made our lives so much easier. No more shortening under the fingernails or messy cookie sheets to clean. This wonder is Von Snedaker's "Magic Baking Sheet," which we purchased at a local kitchen specialty store. It's a 17x14-inch sheet of pliable material that comes rolled up in a tube. You can cut it to fit your favorite cookie sheet, cake pans, or baking dishes. It makes every pan you use it in nonstick; no more greasing or flouring! You can use the magic baking sheet over and over again and it takes only a soapy sponging to clean it. Truly, it's one of those items that, once you use it, you wonder how you ever did without it.

· Favorite gadget #2 is a dough scraper. It's just a piece of metal with a wooden handle across the top. When you're shaping dough, it's great for scraping the dough off the counter and also for cutting it into smaller pieces for rolls, bread sticks, etc. Haven't you seen TV spots where they show great pastry chefs using a dough scraper to manipulate the dough? Honest, that's what you'll feel like, too, when you work with one—a world-renowned bread chef! You'll be buying one of those fancy white hats, next.

· Our most often-used tool is a good serrated bread knife. If you have trouble cutting even slices, consider an electric knife, a fiddlebow knife (see Sources, page 215), or a small, portable food slicer. If you have a large Welbilt or DAK machine and want to cut perfect, round slices, DAK Industries sells a bread holder that will enable you to cut uniform ½-inch thick, round slices.

· We both have citrus trees and like to add citrus peels to many of our breads. For that reason, Linda gets a great deal of use out of a zester. It's a funny-looking little tool, a handle with a flat piece of metal at one end with several tiny holes across the top of the metal piece. It does a good job of removing just the flavorful outer peel and not the bitter white pith underneath. Lois's zester is more unusual; she uses a Microplane rasp. It started out as a carpenter's tool but does a great job in the kitchen, too.

· A pastry brush is invaluable when it comes to bushing melted butter on all those yummy cinnamon-roll doughs or oiling pizza pans.

· If you want to cut back on the oil you use to grease a pan and be good to the environment at the same time, try one of those new spritzers that you can fill with your oil of choice. Just pump it and spray. No more nasty propellants. We're so nuts about them, we now own several. Don't forget to set one aside for your favorite vinaigrette dressing. Rather then drench your salad in too much oil, you can now mist it!

· If you keep a kosher kitchen, order a second bread pan for your machine.

· Keep a roll of plain dental floss handy. When it comes time to slice those cinnamon rolls, instead of crushing them with a knife, place a long strand of dental floss underneath the roll, bring the ends up, cross them, and pull in opposite directions until you cut through the roll.

· At our local warehouse discount club, we discovered the large, rimmed, heavy baking sheets professional bakers use. They're a little larger than a jelly roll pan and work beautifully for all types of breads, rolls, and coffee cakes. Restaurant supply houses also carry them.

· We find it helpful to store things such as honey, molasses, and liquid lecithin in plastic squeeze bottles. (Make sure they were intended for food use.) They should be microwaveable, too. Linda has a row of little plastic honey bear squeeze bottles that greet her every time she opens her bread cupboard.

· Linda pulled her dehydrator out of storage, dusted it off, and put it to use again drying fruits, tomatoes, and fresh herbs for breads. The two appliances make a great duo.

· Salton-Maxim has developed a bread machine that also makes bagels. It boils and bakes 4 bagels at a time in approximately 15 minutes. Someone pass the cream cheese, please.

· Another fun appliance that seems to go hand-in-hand with a bread machine is an electric snackmaker. You can turn a few slices of bread into all kinds of hot sandwiches and tidbits. Butter the outside of the bread slices, fill with anything from pizza ingredients to apple pie filling, close it up to bake, and in just a few minutes it's done! It's a great way to use up those last slices in each loaf. And for those of you with round loaves of bread, DAK Industries has created a sandwich maker for the Welbilt/DAK machine breads.

· The least expensive item on the list: a $1 large aluminum salt shaker with a handle. (It's about 4 inches tall and 2½ inches in diameter.) Fill it with flour and use it for dusting your countertop when you roll out dough. It is also useful for giving country French breads a dusting of flour on top prior to baking.

· If you love crisp French bread, there are side-by-side French baguette pans made of a perforated metal (some are shiny, some are black) that yield the crispest crust possible next to a French bakery.

· We use a similar perforated pan for baking pizzas. It's 14 inches in diameter and produces a wonderful crisp pizza crust . . . no more soft or soggy bottoms.

· Another option for producing crisp French breads and pizza crusts is to bake them on a baking stone. Most gourmet cooking stores carry them.

· If your machine didn't include a measuring spoon, a set that includes a ½ tablespoon measure comes in very handy.

· A good pizza wheel to cut pizzas is a must if you bake your own quite often.

Linda has an el-cheapo model that wobbles so much we should attach training wheels to it.

· You'll notice in our French Bread recipe (page 149) that we suggest letting the dough rise in a cloth-lined, round wicker basket for the most authentic loaf. The basket we used was 7 inches across the bottom, 3½ inches high, and 10 inches across the top. It worked beautifully.

· If you like to check the bread dough often as it kneads and during rising, a timer on a necklace will help you remember to do so when you're busy with other projects.

· Lois has a heavy ball-bearing rolling pin that she covers with a rolling pin cloth. Linda is eyeing it with envy. We've used it many times in our bread machine classes and it works like a charm.

· We've seen crumb boxes in several catalogs. They are the size of a small cutting board with wooden slats across the top. When you slice your bread on it, all the crumbs drop down into the box. There's no mess and they're attractive enough to use as a serving tray on your dining-room table.

· Good French bread is always a hit and we bake a lot of it. A plant mister stored above the oven comes in handy for spraying the bread with water as it bakes, to produce that crispy crust.

· We don't own one yet but we both have our eye on it: a good large, wooden cutting board that hooks over the edge of the counter. They have one in the cooking school where we teach and it's a joy to work on.

· Linda's sister, Debbie, surprised her one Christmas with personalized paper bags that read "Baked especially for you in the oven of . . . [your name]". A large loaf of bread is pictured, also. They are *perfect* for all those gift breads. Miles Kimball still carries them (see page 218). Buy several sets; they go fast!

· King Arthur (see page 216) has various sizes of plastic storage bags for breads, including the hard-to-find bags for the large Panasonic/National loaves.

· Our favorite gift bags for special occasions are the BakerBagz (see Sources, page 218).

· Both Miles Kimball and King Arthur (see pages 218 and 216) sell the shrinking bread keeper, an expandable plastic bread case that keeps bread fresher longer than anything else we've used, even plastic bags. The bread machine loaves fit perfectly. Order two . . . they're inexpensive!

· When Jim remodeled Lois's kitchen, he installed halogen lights under the cupboards above her bread machine. Lois soon discovered that the lights gave off just enough heat to consistently produce taller, lighter loaves. Now she always leaves them on to boost her breads during the cold winter months.

· Lois loves her Thermador warming drawer, too. Besides warming her dinner plates, she also uses it to raise bread dough. She sets the warming oven on low for ten minutes, then turns it off and places the dough inside. Within 30 to 45 minutes, her dough has doubled in size and she swears it bakes up much better than oven-raised loaves.

· No matter how you raise sourdough or French bread doughs, the ideal way to bake them is in La Cloche. It's a clay cooker that comes in both round and oblong shapes. It can be found in gourmet kitchen stores such as Williams-Sonoma or ordered from King Arthur (see page 216). You'll think you've suddenly been transported to a boulevard cafe on the Champs Elysées once you bite into your first loaf baked in La Cloche! It's the only way to produce French bread's thin, crackly crust in your own oven.

· Our friend Bev Janson came up with an alternative to the La Cloche. Remember those large clay cookers that were popular many years ago? Well, if you still have one tucked away in your pantry or garage, time to pull it out, dust it off, and put it to use. You can bake wonderful French/sourdough bread in it! Bev dusts the bottom of the clay cooker and the dough with flour before rising. Thanks, Bev, for the great tip!

· Do you want to keep up with the latest in bread-baking techniques, etc.? Two great newsletters cover all the bases. King Arthur Flour puts out a bi-monthly pamphlet called "The Baking Sheet" which is geared to baking of every sort but also offers at least one bread machine recipe each issue, plus directions on how to convert some of their other bread recipes for your machine. (See Sources page 216 for their address and phone number.) The other is an online newsletter titled *The Bread Digest.* There's both a daily version and a weekly version. The digests are filled with new recipes to try plus a constant exchange of questions and answers for all your bread-baking dilemmas. See our Sources section (page 215) for information on how to subscribe.

6
Recipes

We tested our recipes on fourteen different machines: various models of the Panasonic, Zojirushi, Breadman, Toastmaster, Hitachi, West Bend, Regal, Williams-Sonoma, Betty Crocker, Black and Decker, Welbilt, and DAK. In order to create generic recipes to suit all machines, we have given a range of amounts for ingredients such as liquid, gluten, and yeast. Here are a few suggestions and observations:

1. LIQUIDS: Start with the least amount, observe your dough and listen to your machine as it mixes. If the dough looks dry or stiff or if the machine sounds like it's straining as it kneads, add the extra one or two tablespoons liquid called for in the recipe. In general, with the 1½- and 2-pound recipes, most machines require the maximum amount of liquid called for in the recipe. We found Panasonic, Hitachi, Toastmaster, and Williams-Sonoma bread machines were the exceptions. With the 1-pound recipes, most machines produced better loaves when using the least amount of liquid. The exception was the small 1-pound Welbilt machine. The addition of just one extra tablespoon of liquid to the Welbilt machine often resulted in a taller, lighter loaf.

2. GLUTEN: Gluten is listed as an optional ingredient in several whole-grain recipes. If you prefer a lighter, taller loaf, add the vital wheat gluten—1 tablespoon per cup of flour is usually adequate, though Williams-Sonoma recommends as much as ⅓ cup in some of their recipes. If you add that much gluten, watch the dough as it mixes . . . you'll probably need to add an extra tablespoon or two of liquid as well.

3. YEAST: Most machines used the larger amount of yeast listed in our recipes. With the Toastmaster and the Panasonic SD-BT10P we were able to use less yeast. We also want to remind owners of the older 1½-pound Panasonic SD-BT6P that you will need to double the yeast amount in most recipes.

The recipes are listed as "small," "medium," and "large." The small is the 1-pound loaf that contains approximately 2 cups flour. The medium is the 1½-pound loaf that uses about 3 cups flour. The large is the 2-pound loaf that calls for approximately 4 cups flour. One very important note about the large (2-pound) recipes: Not every "2-pound machine" has a bread pan large enough to accommodate a 2-pound recipe calling for 4 cups flour. Please measure the capacity of your bread pan if you own a 2-pound bread machine. If it holds at least 13 cups water, it should work with the large recipes in this book. (**Note:** Some horizontal 2-pound bread pans work well even though they don't have that large a capacity. We didn't have the same overflow problems with them as we did with the small vertical pans.) If you have a bread pan that holds anything less than 13 cups water, we caution you to *always* start with the medium-size recipe first. In fact, we encourage everyone to try the medium-size loaf first when baking a new recipe. If the medium recipe is a lid-thumper, you'll know not to tempt the fates and try the larger size.

Each recipe can be baked on the standard Bake cycle; however, at the end of each recipe we have noted alternative baking cycles you might prefer to use, if your machine has them. **Important: If the standard Bake cycle on your machine is less than 3 hours and some of the heavier breads aren't baking up tall enough, try switching to the longer Whole Wheat cycle.**

Quick tips for the best results: Always use bread flour when called for in the recipe. Use large-size eggs when a recipe includes eggs. All our recipes were tested with Red Star brand active dry yeast and we recommend using it to achieve the same results. (Buying it in 2-pound bulk packages at warehouse club stores is a wonderful money saver!) Add the ingredients to your bread pan in the order listed. The blurbs at the top of each recipe often emphasize an important step or ingredient, so don't overlook them.

We have included a nutritional analysis at the end of each recipe to be used as a general guideline. The information was calculated on an average 1½-pound loaf containing fourteen ½-inch slices of bread.

We hope you'll find many favorites in the recipes that follow. When you wear this book out, here's one last tip from Linda Caldwell, a very helpful friend to so many of us on the Prodigy network: Kinko's or any other business print shop can spiral bind your favorite, well-worn cookbooks at a reasonable price.

You've read the book, you've learned all our tricks, now it's time to start baking!

Anadama Bread

There's a story that goes along with this classic bread, which dates back to colonial times. A cantankerous New England backwoodsman had a very lazy wife, named Anna, who fed him nothing but cornmeal mush for supper. Night after night he ate cornmeal mush until one evening he couldn't take it any more. He grabbed some flour, molasses, and yeast off the shelf, stirred it into his mush, and put it in the fire to bake. As the loaf baked, he muttered over and over, "Anna, damn her!" That's the origin of the word Anadama.

	SMALL	MEDIUM	LARGE
WATER	¾ to ⅞ cup	1⅛ to 1¼ cups	1½ to 1⅝ cups
MOLASSES	2 tablespoons	3 tablespoons	¼ cup
SALT	1 teaspoon	1½ teaspoons	2 teaspoons
BUTTER OR MARGARINE	1 tablespoon	1½ tablespoons	2 tablespoons
BREAD FLOUR	2 cups	3 cups	4 cups
CORNMEAL	¼ cup	⅓ cup	½ cup
RED STAR BRAND ACTIVE DRY YEAST	1½ teaspoons	2 teaspoons	2½ teaspoons

1. Place all ingredients in bread pan, using the least amount of liquid listed in the recipe. Select Medium Crust setting and press Start.

2. Observe the dough as it kneads. After 5 to 10 minutes, if it appears dry and stiff or if your machine sounds as if it's straining to knead it, add more liquid 1 tablespoon at a time until dough forms a smooth, soft, pliable ball that is slightly tacky to the touch.

3. After the baking cycle ends, remove bread from pan, place on cake rack, and allow to cool 1 hour before slicing.

CRUST: Medium
BAKE CYCLE: Standard
OPTIONAL BAKE CYCLES: Sweet Bread / Delayed Timer

NUTRITIONAL INFORMATION PER SLICE
Calories 130 / Fat 1.5 grams / Carbohydrates 25.4 grams / Protein 3.2 grams / Fiber 1 gram / Sodium 244 milligrams / Cholesterol 0 milligram

Anne and Bill's Apple Oatmeal Bread
with Raisins

*O*atmeal and applesauce combine to make this a lush, rich-tasting loaf. It's a good snack for children and great for breakfast toast.

	SMALL	MEDIUM	LARGE
OLD-FASHIONED ROLLED OATS	⅓ cup	½ cup	⅔ cup
WATER	½ to ⅝ cup	⅝ to ¾ cup	⅞ to 1 cup
UNSWEETENED APPLESAUCE	⅓ cup	½ cup	⅔ cup
SALT	1 teaspoon	1½ teaspoons	1½ teaspoons
BUTTER OR MARGARINE	1 tablespoon	1½ tablespoons	2 tablespoons
BROWN SUGAR	1 tablespoon	2 tablespoons	2 tablespoons
BREAD FLOUR	1¾ cups	2¾ cups	3½ cups
NONFAT DRY MILK POWDER	1 tablespoon	1½ tablespoons	2 tablespoons
RAISINS	¼ cup	⅓ cup	½ cup
GROUND CINNAMON	1 teaspoon	1 teaspoon	2 teaspoons
RED STAR BRAND ACTIVE DRY YEAST	1½ teaspoons	2 teaspoons	2½ teaspoons

1. Place all ingredients in bread pan, using the least amount of liquid listed in the recipe. Select Light Crust setting and press Start.

2. Observe the dough as it kneads. After 5 to 10 minutes, if it appears dry and stiff or if your machine sounds as if it's straining to knead it, add more liquid 1 tablespoon at a time until dough forms a smooth, soft, pliable ball that is slightly tacky to the touch.

3. After the baking cycle ends, remove bread from pan, place on cake rack, and allow to cool 1 hour before slicing.

CRUST: Light

BAKE CYCLE: Standard

OPTIONAL BAKE CYCLES: Whole Wheat / Sweet Bread / Raisin Nut / Delayed Timer

---

NUTRITIONAL INFORMATION PER SLICE

Calories 114 / Fat .5 grams / Carbohydrates 23.8 grams / Protein 3.4 grams / Fiber 1.3 grams / Sodium 232 milligrams / Cholesterol .1 milligrams

Ann's Bierocks

Ann Slaybaugh, Special Ed teacher and friend, often claimed she wasn't much of a cook. We found it hard to believe when she shared recipes like this one and also took to the bread machine like a pro! These buns are filled with hamburger, cabbage, cheese, and onion—perfect to have on hand for a light lunch or to take along on a camping trip. This basic recipe is fun to play with when you're in a creative mood.

	SMALL	MEDIUM	LARGE
DOUGH			
WATER	½ cup	¾ cup	¾ cup
EGG	1	1	2
OIL	3 tablespoons	¼ cup	6 tablespoons
SALT	½ teaspoon	1 teaspoon	1½ teaspoons
SUGAR	3 tablespoons	¼ cup	6 tablespoons
ALL-PURPOSE FLOUR	2 cups	3 cups	4 cups
RED STAR BRAND ACTIVE DRY YEAST	2 teaspoons	2 teaspoons	2½ teaspoons
FILLING			
GROUND BEEF	1½ pounds	2 pounds	2½ pounds
CHOPPED ONION	½ cup	¾ cup	1 cup
CHOPPED CABBAGE	1½ cups	2 cups	2½ cups
SALT AND PEPPER	to taste	to taste	to taste
GRATED CHEDDAR CHEESE	½ cup (2 ounces)	¾ cup (3 ounces)	1 cup (4 ounces)
MELTED BUTTER OR MARGARINE	2 tablespoons	2 tablespoons	3 tablespoons

1. Place all ingredients in bread pan, select Dough setting, and press Start.

2. Meanwhile, in a medium skillet, brown the ground beef. Drain off all grease. Return skillet to heat and add the onion, cabbage, salt, and pepper. Cover and cook on

low heat for 15 minutes until the cabbage is tender. Stir in the cheese. Remove the mixture from heat and set aside.

3. When the dough has risen long enough, the machine will beep. Turn off bread machine, remove bread pan, and turn out dough onto a lightly floured countertop or cutting board. Gently roll and stretch dough into a 12-inch rope.

For the Small Recipe

With a sharp knife, divide the dough into 12 pieces.

For the Medium Recipe

With a sharp knife, divide the dough into 18 pieces.

For the Large Recipe

With a sharp knife, divide the dough into 24 pieces.

4. Grease a large baking sheet.

5. With a rolling pin, roll each piece into a 5-inch circle. Place a heaping ¼ cup of filling mixture in the center of each circle. Pull the edges up to meet in the center and pinch the dough together well to seal. Place on prepared baking sheet, sealed-side down. Cover and let rise in a warm oven 30 to 45 minutes until doubled in size. (*Hint:* To warm oven slightly, turn oven on Warm setting for 1 minute, then turn it off, and place covered dough in oven to rise. Remove pan from oven before pre-heating.)

6. Preheat oven to 350°F. Before baking, brush each bun with the melted butter. Bake 20 minutes until golden brown.

7. Remove from oven and serve warm.

Small recipe yields 12 buns
Medium recipe yields 18 buns
Large recipe yields 24 buns

BAKE CYCLE: Dough

NUTRITIONAL INFORMATION PER BUN
Calories 335 / Fat 19.1 grams / Carbohydrates 22.2 grams / Protein 17.8 grams / Fiber 1.1 grams / Sodium 231 milligrams / Cholesterol 73.5 milligrams

Applesauce Rye Bread

The combination of applesauce, rye, and molasses makes for a moist, dark bread that's perfect for breakfast . . . a nice way to start the day.

	SMALL	MEDIUM	LARGE
SWEETENED APPLESAUCE	¾ cup	1 cup	1¼ cups
WATER	⅛ cup	¼ to ⅜ cup + 1 tablespoon	½ to ⅝ cup
MOLASSES	1½ tablespoons	2 tablespoons	3 tablespoons
SALT	½ teaspoon	½ teaspoon	1 teaspoon
BUTTER OR MARGARINE	1½ tablespoons	2 tablespoons	3 tablespoons
BREAD FLOUR	2 cups	2¾ cups	3 cups
RYE FLOUR	½ cup	1 cup	1½ cups
VITAL WHEAT GLUTEN, OPTIONAL	2 tablespoons	3 tablespoons	¼ cup
CARAWAY SEEDS	2 teaspoons	1 tablespoon	4 teaspoons
RED STAR BRAND ACTIVE DRY YEAST	1½ teaspoons	2 teaspoons	2½ teaspoons

1. Place all ingredients in bread pan, using the least amount of liquid listed in the recipe. Select Medium Crust setting and press Start.

2. Observe the dough as it kneads. After 5 to 10 minutes, if it appears dry and stiff or if your machine sounds as if it's straining to knead it, add more liquid 1 tablespoon at a time until dough forms a smooth, soft, pliable ball that is slightly tacky to the touch.

3. After the baking cycle ends, remove bread from pan, place on cake rack, and allow to cool 1 hour before slicing.

CRUST: Medium

BAKE CYCLE: Standard

OPTIONAL BAKE CYCLES: Whole Wheat / Sweet Bread / Delayed Timer

---

NUTRITIONAL INFORMATION PER SLICE
Calories 153 / Fat 2.1 grams / Carbohydrates 29.8 grams / Protein 3.5 grams / Fiber 2.2 grams / Sodium 92 milligrams / Cholesterol 4.4 milligrams

Black Forest Pumpernickel

This is a dark bread with that fabulous, distinctive rye flavor. Pair this soul-satisfying bread with thin slices of ham and cheese or a mug of homemade potato soup.

	SMALL	MEDIUM	LARGE
WATER	¾ to ⅞ cup	1⅛ to 1¼ cups	1½ to 1⅝ cups
OIL	1 tablespoon	1½ tablespoons	2 tablespoons
MOLASSES	3 tablespoons	⅓ cup	6 tablespoons
SALT	1 teaspoon	1½ teaspoons	2 teaspoons
BREAD FLOUR	⅔ cup	1½ cups	1⅓ cups
RYE FLOUR	⅔ cup	1 cup	1⅓ cups
WHOLE WHEAT FLOUR	⅔ cup	1 cup	1⅓ cups
VITAL WHEAT GLUTEN	2 tablespoons	3 tablespoons	¼ cup
COCOA POWDER	2 tablespoons	3 tablespoons	¼ cup
CARAWAY SEEDS	2 teaspoons	1 tablespoon	4 teaspoons
RED STAR BRAND ACTIVE DRY YEAST	1½ teaspoons	2 teaspoons	2½ teaspoons

I. Place all ingredients in bread pan, using the least amount of liquid listed in the recipe. Select Medium Crust setting and Whole Wheat cycle. Press Start.

2. Observe the dough as it kneads. After 5 to 10 minutes, if it appears dry and stiff or if your machine sounds as if it's straining to knead it, add more liquid 1 tablespoon at a time until dough forms a smooth, soft, pliable ball that is slightly tacky to the touch.

3. After the baking cycle ends, remove bread from pan, place on cake rack, and allow to cool 1 hour before slicing.

CRUST: Medium

BAKE CYCLE: Whole Wheat

OPTIONAL BAKE CYCLES: Standard / Sweet Bread / Delayed Timer

NUTRITIONAL INFORMATION PER SLICE
Calories 139 / Fat 2.2 grams / Carbohydrates 27.1 grams / Protein 3.7 grams / Fiber 3.1 grams / Sodium 231 milligrams / Cholesterol 0 milligram

Butterhorn Rolls

*M*ake these rolls just once and they will become one of your favorites. They look impressive but they're deceptively simple to make because the dough is so easy to handle. They're rich, tender rolls—perfect for company dinners or festive holiday meals.

	SMALL	MEDIUM	LARGE
MILK	½ cup	¾ cup	⅞ cup
EGG	1	1	2
OIL	¼ cup	⅓ cup	½ cup
SALT	½ teaspoon	1 teaspoon	1½ teaspoons
SUGAR	¼ cup	⅓ cup	½ cup
ALL-PURPOSE FLOUR	2 cups	3 cups	4 cups
RED STAR BRAND ACTIVE DRY YEAST	1½ teaspoons	1½ teaspoons	2 teaspoons
MELTED BUTTER OR MARGARINE	1 tablespoon	1½ tablespoons	2 tablespoons

1. Place all ingredients except melted butter in bread pan, select Dough setting, and press Start.

2. When the dough has risen long enough, the machine will beep. Turn off bread machine, remove bread pan, and turn out dough onto a lightly floured countertop or cutting board. Shape dough into a log.

For the Small Recipe
With a sharp knife, divide dough into 2 pieces; roll each piece into a ball.

For the Medium Recipe
With a sharp knife, divide dough into 3 pieces; roll each piece into a ball.

For the Large Recipe
With a sharp knife, divide dough into 4 pieces; roll each piece into a ball.

3. With a rolling pin, roll each ball, one at a time, into a 9-inch circle. With a sharp knife or pizza cutter, divide each circle into 8 wedges, as if cutting a pizza. Starting at the wide end, roll up each wedge toward the point. Place rolls on an ungreased baking sheet, point-side underneath. Cover and let rise in a warm oven 30 to 45 minutes until double in side. (**Hint:** To warm oven slightly, turn oven on Warm setting for 1 minute, then turn it off, and place covered dough in oven to rise. Remove pan from oven before preheating.)

4. Preheat oven to 375 F. Brush rolls lightly with melted butter. Bake for 12 to 15 minutes until golden. Remove from oven and serve warm.

Small recipe yields 16 rolls
Medium recipe yields 24 rolls
Large recipe yields 32 rolls

BAKE CYCLE: Dough

NUTRITIONAL INFORMATION PER ROLL
Calories 107 / Fat 4.2 grams / Carbohydrates 15.1 grams / Protein 2.2 grams / Fiber .5 gram / Sodium 104 milligrams / Cholesterol 9.2 milligrams

---

Buttermilk Cracked-Wheat Bread

*R*aw *cracked wheat adds a crunchy texture to this noteworthy whole wheat bread. It's not as tall as some loaves, but it's just as delicious. Serve it proudly with dinner or use it for sandwiches.*

	SMALL	MEDIUM	LARGE
CRACKED WHEAT	⅓ cup	½ cup	⅔ cup
BUTTERMILK	⅞ to 1 cup	1⅜ to 1½ cups	2¼ to 2⅜ cups
HONEY	1½ tablespoons	2 tablespoons	3 tablespoons
SALT	1 teaspoon	1½ teaspoons	2 teaspoons
SHORTENING	1 tablespoon	1 tablespoon	2 tablespoons
WHOLE WHEAT FLOUR	1⅓ cups	2 cups	2⅔ cups
BREAD FLOUR	⅔ cup	1 cup	1⅓ cups
VITAL WHEAT GLUTEN, OPTIONAL	2 tablespoons	3 tablespoons to ⅓ cup	4 tablespoons
RED STAR BRAND ACTIVE DRY YEAST	1½ teaspoons	2 teaspoons	2½ teaspoons

I. Place all ingredients in bread pan, using the least amount of liquid listed in the recipe. Select Medium Crust setting and Whole Wheat cycle. Press Start.

2. Observe the dough as it kneads. After 5 to 10 minutes, if it appears dry and stiff or if your machine sounds as if it's straining to knead it, add more liquid 1 tablespoon at a time until dough forms a smooth, soft, pliable ball that is slightly tacky to the touch.

3. After the baking cycle ends, remove bread from pan, place on cake rack, and allow to cool 1 hour before slicing.

CRUST: Medium
BAKE CYCLE: Whole Wheat
OPTIONAL BAKE CYCLES: Standard / Sweet Bread

NUTRITIONAL INFORMATION PER SLICE
Calories 136 / Fat 1.6 grams / Carbohydrates 26.7 grams / Protein 4.8 grams / Fiber 3.6 grams / Sodium 256 milligrams / Cholesterol .9 milligrams

Buttermilk Honey Bran Bread

This bakes up into a lovely, tall loaf flecked with bran that has a wholesome taste.

	SMALL	MEDIUM	LARGE
MILLER'S BRAN	⅓ cup	½ cup	⅔ cup
BUTTERMILK	⅞ to 1 cup	1¼ to 1⅜ cups	1⅝ to 1¾ cups
HONEY	2 tablespoons	3 tablespoons	¼ cup
SALT	¾ teaspoon	1½ teaspoons	1½ teaspoons
BUTTER OR MARGARINE	1 tablespoon	1½ tablespoons	2 tablespoons
BREAD FLOUR	2 cups	3 cups	4 cups
RED STAR BRAND ACTIVE DRY YEAST	1½ teaspoons	2 teaspoons	2½ teaspoons

1. Place all ingredients in bread pan, using the least amount of liquid listed in the recipe. Select Medium Crust setting and press Start.

2. Observe the dough as it kneads. After 5 to 10 minutes, if it appears dry and stiff or if your machine sounds as if it's straining to knead it, add more liquid 1 tablespoon at a time until dough forms a smooth, soft, pliable ball that is slightly tacky to the touch.

3. After the baking cycle ends, remove bread from pan, place on cake rack, and allow to cool 1 hour before slicing.

CRUST: Medium

BAKE CYCLE: Standard

OPTIONAL BAKE CYCLES: Sweet Bread / Rapid Bake

NUTRITIONAL INFORMATION PER SLICE
Calories 136 / Fat 1.8 grams / Carbohydrates 26.6 grams / Protein 3.9 grams / Fiber 1.4 grams / Sodium 263 milligrams / Cholesterol 4.1 milligrams

Caraway Rye Pan Rolls

*T*hese are rich, tender pan rolls—the perfect accompaniment to hearty split pea soup or a pork chop and sauerkraut supper.

	SMALL	MEDIUM	LARGE
WATER	⅔ cup	¾ cup	1¼ cups
SOUR CREAM	⅓ cup	½ cup	⅔ cup
SALT	1½ teaspoons	2 teaspoons	2 teaspoons
SUGAR	2 teaspoons	1 tablespoon	4 teaspoons
ALL-PURPOSE FLOUR	1½ cups	2 cups	3 cups
RYE FLOUR	¾ cup	1 cup	1½ cups
CARAWAY SEEDS	2 teaspoons	1 tablespoon	4 teaspoons
RED STAR BRAND ACTIVE DRY YEAST	1½ teaspoons	1½ teaspoons	2 teaspoons

1. Place all ingredients in bread pan, select Dough setting, and press Start.

2. When the dough has risen long enough, the machine will beep. Turn off bread machine, remove bread pan, and turn out dough onto a lightly floured countertop or cutting board. (*Note:* This is a very sticky dough, so keep your hands and the countertop well covered with flour.) Gently roll and stretch dough into an 18-inch rope.

For the Small Recipe
Grease one 9-inch round or square cake pan. With a sharp knife, divide dough into 9 pieces; roll each into a ball and place in pan.

For the Medium Recipe
Grease a 9x13x2-inch pan. With a sharp knife, divide dough into 12 pieces; roll each into a ball and place in pan.

For the Large Recipe
Grease two 9-inch round or square cake pans. With a sharp knife, divide dough into 18 pieces; roll each into a ball and place 9 in each pan.

3. Cover and let rise in a warm oven 30 to 45 minutes until doubled in size. (*Hint:* to warm oven slightly, turn oven on Warm setting for 1 minute, then turn it off, and place covered dough in oven to rise. Remove pan from oven before preheating.)

4. Preheat oven to 400°F. Bake rolls for 18 minutes until golden. Remove from oven and serve warm.

Small recipe yields 9 rolls
Medium recipe yields 12 rolls
Large recipe yields 18 rolls

BAKE CYCLE: Dough

NUTRITIONAL INFORMATION PER ROLL
Calories 67 / Fat 1.2 grams / Carbohydrates 12.1 grams / Protein 1.7 grams / Fiber 1 gram / Sodium 181 milligrams / Cholesterol 2.1 milligrams

---

Chicken Broccoli Pockets

*I*f you're lucky enough to have any of these left over, pop them in the freezer and you'll have a handy lunch to grab on those mornings you're running late for work. Reheat in a microwave oven for 6 to 7 minutes on *MEDIUM* power.

	SMALL	MEDIUM	LARGE
DOUGH			
WATER	⅜ cup	⅜ cup	¾ cup
MILK	⅜ cup	⅝ cup	⅝ cup
SALT	1 teaspoon	1½ teaspoons	2 teaspoons
BUTTER OR MARGARINE	1 tablespoon	1½ tablespoons	2 tablespoons
SUGAR	2 tablespoons	3 tablespoons	¼ cup
BREAD FLOUR	2 cups	3 cups	4 cups
RED STAR BRAND ACTIVE DRY YEAST	1½ teaspoons	1½ teaspoons	2 teaspoons
FILLING			
CONDENSED CREAM OF CHICKEN SOUP	⅔ cup	¾ cup	1⅓ cups
CHOPPED, COOKED CHICKEN	1⅓ cups	2 cups	2⅔ cups

(continued)

FROZEN, CHOPPED BROCCOLI, THAWED AND DRAINED	1⅓ cups	2 cups	2⅔ cups
GRATED MOZZARELLA CHEESE	¾ cup (3 ounces)	1 cup (4 ounces)	1½ cups (6 ounces)
CHOPPED ONION	3 tablespoons	½ cup	6 tablespoons

1. Place all ingredients in bread pan, select Dough setting, and press Start.

2. Meanwhile, in a medium bowl, combine the soup, chicken, broccoli, cheese, and onion; cover and refrigerate until needed.

3. When the dough has risen long enough, the machine will beep. Turn off bread machine, remove bread pan, and turn out dough onto a lightly floured countertop or cutting board. Shape dough into a log.

4. Grease a large baking sheet.

For the Small Recipe
   With a sharp knife, divide dough into 6 pieces.

For the Medium Recipe
   With a sharp knife, divide dough into 9 pieces.

For the Large Recipe
   With a sharp knife, divide dough into 12 pieces.

5. With a rolling pin, roll each piece into a 6-inch circle. Place approximately ½ cup of filling on one side of circle and spread to within ½ inch of the edge. Fold other half of dough over filling. Seal well by pressing edges together with the tines of a fork. With same fork, prick top of each pocket a few times. Place pockets on prepared baking sheet.

6. Preheat oven to 375°F. Bake pockets for 25 to 30 minutes until golden brown. Remove from oven and serve warm. Leftovers can be frozen.

Small recipe yields 6 pockets
Medium recipe yields 9 pockets
Large recipe yields 12 pockets

BAKE CYCLE: Dough

NUTRITIONAL INFORMATION PER POCKET
Calories 371 / Fat 11.3 grams / Carbohydrates 46.1 grams / Protein 20.5 grams / Fiber 2.9 grams / Sodium 738 milligrams / Cholesterol 52.8 milligrams

Chili Burgers

You can make these "burgers" as mild or as spicy as you desire with your choice of cheese. For a mild flavor, choose plain Monterey Jack cheese; for a little more "heat," select a mild green chile pepper cheese; for a near-volcanic heat (limited to the brave and daring), try jalapeño pepper cheese.

	SMALL	MEDIUM	LARGE
DOUGH			
MILK	¼ cup	⅜ cup	⅜ cup
WATER	¼ cup	⅜ to ½ cup	⅜ cup
EGG	1	1	2
SALT	1 teaspoon	1½ teaspoons	2 teaspoons
SHORTENING	2 tablespoons	3 tablespoons	¼ cup
SUGAR	2 tablespoons	3 tablespoons	¼ cup
ALL-PURPOSE FLOUR	2 cups	3 cups	4 cups
RED STAR BRAND ACTIVE DRY YEAST	2 teaspoons	2 teaspoons	2½ teaspoons
FILLING			
GROUND BEEF	1 pound	1 pound	2 pounds
LARGE ONION, CHOPPED	½ onion	¾ onion	1 onion
CHILI POWDER	1½ teaspoons	2 teaspoons	1 tablespoon
SALT	½ teaspoon	½ teaspoon	1 teaspoon
PEPPER	¼ teaspoon	¼ teaspoon	½ teaspoon
GRATED MONTEREY JACK CHEESE, MILD GREEN CHILE PEPPER CHEESE, OR JALAPEÑO PEPPER CHEESE	1 cup (4 ounces)	1½ cups (6 ounces)	2 cups (8 ounces)
15-OUNCE CAN CHILI BEANS, DRAINED	1	2	2
MELTED BUTTER OR MARGARINE	2 tablespoons	2 tablespoons	3 tablespoons

I. Place dough ingredients in bread pan, select Dough setting, and press Start.

2. Meanwhile, in a large skillet, cook ground beef and onion over medium heat until meat is no longer pink. Drain off the grease. Reduce heat to low, return skillet to heat, and add the chili powder, salt, pepper, cheese, and beans. Stir gently until beans are heated through, about 5 minutes. Remove skillet from heat; set aside.

3. When the dough has risen long enough, the machine will beep. Turn off bread machine, remove bread pan, and turn out dough onto a lightly floured countertop or cutting board. Gently roll and stretch dough into a 12-inch rope.

For the Small Recipe
With a sharp knife, divide dough into 12 pieces.

For the Medium Recipe
With a sharp knife, divide dough into 18 pieces.

For the Large Recipe
With a sharp knife, divide dough into 24 pieces.

4. Grease a baking sheet. Preheat oven to 400°F.

5. With a rolling pin, roll each piece into a 5-inch circle. Place ⅓ cup of filling mixture in the center of each circle. Pull the edges up to meet in the center and pinch dough together well to seal. Place on prepared baking sheet, sealed-side down.

6. Bake for 15 to 20 minutes until brown. Remove from oven and brush with melted butter. Serve warm. These freeze well in a plastic bag for up to 3 months. To reheat, place in a 325 F oven for 30 minutes or microwave on HIGH for 1½ to 2 minutes.

Small recipe yields 12 burgers
Medium recipe yields 18 burgers
Large recipe yields 24 burgers

BAKE CYCLE: Dough

NUTRITIONAL INFORMATION PER SLICE
Calories 304 / Fat 13.8 grams / Carbohydrates 29.3 grams / Protein 15.2 grams / Fiber 4.8 grams / Sodium 556 milligrams / Cholesterol 48.3 milligrams

---

Christy's Christmas Trees

*T*his is a scrumptious coffee cake that even young children can take part in creating. It's a thoughtful gift during the holiday season, perfect for breakfast
Christmas morning or for a Christmas Eve family gathering.

	SMALL	MEDIUM	LARGE
DOUGH			
BUTTERMILK	⅝ cup	⅞ cup	⅞ cup
EGG	1	1	2
SALT	1 teaspoon	1 teaspoon	2 teaspoons
BUTTER OR MARGARINE	3 tablespoons	4 tablespoons	6 tablespoons
SUGAR	3 tablespoons	¼ cup	6 tablespoons
ALL-PURPOSE FLOUR	2 cups	3 cups	4 cups
RED STAR BRAND ACTIVE DRY YEAST	1½ teaspoons	1½ teaspoons	2 teaspoons
ICING			
POWDERED SUGAR	⅔ cup	1 cup	1⅓ cups
MILK OR EGGNOG	2 to 3 teaspoons	1 to 1½ tablespoons	5 teaspoons
VANILLA	¼ teaspoon	½ teaspoon	¾ teaspoon
GREEN FOOD COLORING	A few drops	A few drops	A few drops
GARNISH			
CINNAMON RED HOTS	For decoration	For decoration	For decoration

1. Place dough ingredients in bread pan, select Dough setting, and press Start.

2. When the dough has risen long enough, the machine will beep. Turn off bread
machine, remove bread pan, and turn out dough onto a lightly floured countertop
or cutting board. Grease a large baking sheet(s).

For the Small Recipe

Gently roll and stretch dough into an 11-inch rope. With a sharp knife, divide the dough into 11 pieces. Roll each piece into a ball and place it on a greased baking sheet in the shape of a tree, spaced about ½ inch apart: 4 balls for the bottom row, 3 balls for the next row, 2 balls for the next row, and 1 ball at the top. Gently roll the remaining ball into a thick rope and shape it into an "S" to form the tree trunk.

GREASED BAKING SHEET

SPACE ABOUT ½"APART

2 BALLS ROLLED MAKE THE TRUNK

Variation:

This recipe makes 1 medium Christmas tree coffee cake. To create 2 or 4 smaller trees, simply divide the dough into 2 or 4 pieces initially and then follow the directions for dividing up the dough and shaping each tree.

For the Medium Recipe

Gently roll and stretch dough into a 17-inch rope. With a sharp knife, divide the dough into 17 pieces. Roll each piece into a ball and place it on a greased baking sheet in the shape of a tree, spaced about ½ inch apart: 5 balls for the bottom row, 4 balls for the next row, 3 balls for the next row, 2 balls for the next row, and 1 ball at the top. Combine the remaining 2 balls into 1 large ball, gently roll it into a thick rope, and shape it into an "S" to form the tree trunk.

Variation:

This recipe makes 1 medium Christmas tree coffee cake. To create 2 or 4 smaller trees, simply divide the dough into 2 or 4 pieces initially and then follow the directions for dividing up the dough and shaping each tree.

For the Large Recipe

With a sharp knife, divide dough in half. Gently roll and stretch dough into two 11-inch ropes. With a sharp knife, divide the dough into 11 pieces. Roll each piece into a ball and place it on a greased baking sheet in the shape of a tree, spaced about ½ inch apart: 4 balls for the bottom row, 3 balls for the next row, 2 balls for the next row, and 1 ball at the top. Gently roll the remaining ball into a thick rope and shape it into an "S" to form the tree trunk. Repeat with the other rope and place on a second greased baking sheet.

VARIATION:

This recipe makes 2 medium Christmas tree coffee cakes. To create 4, 6, or 8 smaller trees, simply divide the dough into 4, 6, or 8 pieces initially and then follow the directions for dividing up the dough and shaping each tree.

3. Cover and let rise in a warm oven 30 to 45 minutes until doubled in size. (*Hint:* to warm oven slightly, turn oven on Warm setting for 1 minute, then turn it off, and place covered dough in oven to rise. Remove pans from oven before preheating.) Preheat oven to 375°F.

4. Bake coffee cake(s) 20 to 25 minutes until golden. Cool on cake rack.

5. When the coffee cake(s) is cooled, in a small bowl, combine the icing ingredients, adding enough liquid to make the icing thin enough to spread over the coffee cake. Spread each roll with icing, then decorate with cinnamon red hot candies.

Small and medium recipes yield 1 Christmas tree coffee cake
Large recipe yields 2 Christmas tree coffee cakes

BAKE CYCLE: Dough

NUTRITIONAL INFORMATION PER ROLL
Calories 149 / Fat 3.4 grams / Carbohydrates 26.3 grams / Protein 3.2 grams / Fiber .7 gram / Sodium 166 milligrams / Cholesterol 20.5 milligrams

---

VARIATION:

This recipe is really too good to be used only once a year at Christmas. We suggest you try it on other holidays, with other shapes and different icing colors. Some that come to mind are "Old Glory" with red, white, and blue icing on the 4th of July; a large red heart for Valentine's Day; a green shamrock for St. Patrick's Day; some cute little teddy bears or even that well-known, large, purple dinosaur for a child's birthday. With just a little thought, you'll come up with many, many more ideas.

Country Rye Bread Sticks

They may be funny looking, but these mild rye bread sticks taste mighty fine.

	SMALL	MEDIUM	LARGE
WATER	¾ cup	1 cup	1¼ cups
SALT	½ teaspoon	½ teaspoon	¾ teaspoon
BUTTER OR MARGARINE	1½ tablespoons	2 tablespoons	3 tablespoons
SUGAR	1½ tablespoons	2 tablespoons	3 tablespoons
BREAD FLOUR	1 cup	1½ cups	2 cups
RYE FLOUR	⅔ cup	1 cup	1⅓ cups
WHOLE WHEAT FLOUR	⅓ cup	½ cup	⅔ cup
CARAWAY SEEDS	1 teaspoon	2 teaspoons	2 teaspoons
RED STAR BRAND ACTIVE DRY YEAST	1½ teaspoons	1½ teaspoons	2 teaspoons

1. Place dough ingredients in bread pan, select Dough setting, and press Start.

2. When the dough has risen long enough, the machine will beep. Turn off bread machine, remove bread pan, and turn out dough onto a lightly floured countertop or cutting board. Shape dough into 6-inch square.

3. Grease two 12x6x1-inch baking sheets. Preheat oven to 350° F.

For the Small Recipe
With a rolling pin, roll dough into a 12x6-inch rectangle. With a pizza wheel, cut dough crosswise into 24 half-inch-wide strips.

For the Medium Recipe
With a sharp knife, cut dough in half. With a rolling pin, roll each piece into a 8x6-inch rectangle. With a pizza wheel, cut dough crosswise into 16 half-inch-wide strips.

For the Large Recipe
With a sharp knife cut dough in half. With a rolling pin, roll each half into a

12x6-inch rectangle. With a pizza wheel, cut dough crosswise into 24 half-inch-wide strips.

4. Roll and stretch each piece into a 16-inch-long stick; place on prepared baking sheets.

5. Bake bread sticks for 20 to 25 minutes. Remove from oven; remove bread sticks from pans and cool on wire racks. Once cool, store at room temperature in plastic bags. They will stay fresh for 3 or 4 days.

Small recipe yields 24 bread sticks
Medium recipe yields 32 bread sticks
Large recipe yields 48 bread sticks

BAKE CYCLE: Dough

NUTRITIONAL INFORMATION PER BREAD STICK
Calories 50 / Fat .9 gram / Carbohydrates 9.2 grams / Protein 1.2 grams / Fiber .9 gram / Sodium 40 milligrams / Cholesterol 1.9 milligrams

---

Dawn's Vanilla Raisin Bread

A student in one of our classes, Dawn Fletcher, gave us the idea of soaking raisins in vanilla, which inspired us to create this bread. This bread bakes up quite high in some machines so keep an eye on it the first time you make it. If you want to make this luscious bread on the spur of the moment, combine the raisins and vanilla, then microwave on HIGH for 1 minute, rather than soaking them for an hour. (Note: For a stronger vanilla flavor, reserve the vanilla drained from the raisins and use it as part of your liquid. If you plan to bake this bread often, use an inexpensive vanilla.)

	SMALL	MEDIUM	LARGE
RAISINS	½ cup	⅔ cup	1 cup
VANILLA EXTRACT	2 tablespoons	3 tablespoons	¼ cup
BUTTERMILK	¾ cup	1⅛ to 1¼ cups	1⅜ to 1½ cups
EGG	omit	1	1
SALT	¾ teaspoon	1 teaspoon	1½ teaspoons
BUTTER OR MARGARINE	2 tablespoons	3 tablespoons	4 tablespoons
SUGAR	1½ tablespoons	2 tablespoons	3 tablespoons
BREAD FLOUR	2 cups	3½ cups	4½ cups
RED STAR BRAND ACTIVE DRY YEAST	1½ teaspoons	2 teaspoons	2 teaspoons

1. Soak raisins in vanilla for at least 1 hour.

2. Drain raisins well. Place all ingredients in bread pan, using the least amount of liquid listed in the recipe. Select Light Crust setting and press Start.

3. Observe the dough as it kneads. After 5 to 10 minutes, if it appears dry and stiff or if your machine sounds as if it's straining to knead it, add more liquid 1 tablespoon at a time until dough forms a smooth, soft, pliable ball that is slightly tacky to the touch.

4. After the baking cycle ends, remove bread from pan, place on cake rack, and allow to cool 1 hour before slicing.

CRUST: Light

BAKE CYCLE: Standard

OPTIONAL BAKE CYCLES: Whole Wheat / Sweet Bread / Raisin Nut

NUTRITIONAL INFORMATION PER SLICE
Calories 180 / Fat 3.3 grams / Carbohydrates 32.8 grams / Protein 4.7 grams / Fiber 1.4 grams / Sodium 200 milligrams / Cholesterol 22.6 milligrams

DeDe's Buttermilk Bread

*T*his bread is by far the most popular from our first book, Bread Machine
Magic. *Two slices from this moist, rich, and tender loaf will make any sandwich exceptional.*

	SMALL	MEDIUM	LARGE
BUTTERMILK	⅞ to 1 cup	1⅛ to 1¼ cups	1½ to 1⅝ cups
HONEY	2 tablespoons	3 tablespoons	¼ cup
SALT	1 teaspoon	1½ teaspoons	2 teaspoons
BUTTER OR MARGARINE	1 tablespoon	1 tablespoon	2 tablespoons
BREAD FLOUR	2 cups	3 cups	4 cups
RED STAR BRAND ACTIVE DRY YEAST	1½ teaspoons	2 teaspoons	2½ teaspoons

I. Place all ingredients in bread pan, using the least amount of liquid listed in the
recipe. Select Light Crust setting and press Start.

2. Observe the dough as it kneads. After 5 to 10 minutes, if it appears dry and stiff or
if your machine sounds as if it's straining to knead it, add more liquid 1 tablespoon
at a time until dough forms a smooth, soft, pliable ball that is slightly tacky to the
touch.

3. After the baking cycle ends, remove bread from pan, place on cake rack, and allow to cool 1 hour before slicing.

CRUST: Light
BAKE CYCLE: Standard
OPTIONAL BAKE CYCLES: Sweet Bread

NUTRITIONAL INFORMATION PER SLICE
Calories 127 / Fat 1.3 grams / Carbohydrates 25.1 grams / Protein 3.5 grams / Fiber .8 gram /
Sodium 257 milligrams / Cholesterol 2.9 milligrams

Dennis's Multigrain Bread

*D*ennis, Linda's husband, raves about this bread every time he has a slice so it was fitting to name it after him. Any multigrain cereal—four, seven, nine, or twelve grain—may be used in this full-bodied bread. Arrowhead Mills and Stone-buhr are two companies that produce and package this coarse-meal cereal. Do not use the version sold in grocery stores that resembles cornflakes.

	SMALL	MEDIUM	LARGE
BUTTERMILK	⅜ cup	¾ cup	¾ cup
WATER	⅛ cup	⅜ to ½ cup	⅜ to ½ cup
EGG	1	1	2
OIL	1½ tablespoons	2 tablespoons	3 tablespoons
HONEY	1½ tablespoons	2 tablespoons	3 tablespoons
SALT	1 teaspoon	1½ teaspoons	2 teaspoons
WHOLE WHEAT FLOUR	1⅔ cups	2½ cups	3⅓ cups
MULTIGRAIN CEREAL	⅓ cup	½ cup	⅔ cup
RAW, UNSALTED SUNFLOWER SEEDS	3 tablespoons	¼ cup	6 tablespoons
VITAL WHEAT GLUTEN	2 tablespoons	3 tablespoons	¼ cup
RED STAR BRAND ACTIVE DRY YEAST	1½ teaspoons	2 teaspoons	2½ teaspoons

1. Place all ingredients in bread pan, using the least amount of liquid listed in the recipe. Select Medium Crust setting and press Start.

2. Observe the dough as it kneads. After 5 to 10 minutes, if it appears dry and stiff or if your machine sounds as if it's straining to knead it, add more liquid 1 tablespoon at a time until dough forms a smooth, soft, pliable ball that is slightly tacky to the touch.

3. After the baking cycle ends, remove bread from pan, place on cake rack, and allow to cool 1 hour before slicing.

CRUST: Medium

BAKE CYCLE: Whole Wheat

OPTIONAL BAKE CYCLES: Standard / Sweet Bread / Raisin Nut

NUTRITIONAL INFORMATION PER SLICE
Calories 143 / Fat 4.2 grams / Carbohydrates 22.5 grams / Protein 5.8 grams / Fiber 3.1 grams / Sodium 248 milligrams / Cholesterol 15.7 milligrams

Egg Bread

Need a bread for sandwiches? Here's the perfect companion for anything from tuna to cheese. The eggs give it a rich, velvety taste and texture. We like to keep a loaf in the freezer for Sunday morning's French toast.

	SMALL	MEDIUM	LARGE
MILK	½ to ⅝ cup + 1 tablespoon	¾ to ⅞ cup	1 to 1⅛ cups
EGG	1	2	3
SALT	1 teaspoon	1½ teaspoons	2 teaspoons
BUTTER OR MARGARINE	2 tablespoons	3 tablespoons	4 tablespoons
SUGAR	3 tablespoons	¼ cup	¼ cup
BREAD FLOUR	2 cups	3 cups	4 cups
RED STAR BRAND ACTIVE DRY YEAST	1½ teaspoons	2 teaspoons	2½ teaspoons

1. Place all ingredients in bread pan, using the least amount of liquid listed in the recipe. Select Light Crust setting and press Start.

2. Observe the dough as it kneads. After 5 to 10 minutes, if it appears dry and stiff or if your machine sounds as if it's straining to knead it, add more liquid 1 tablespoon at a time until dough forms a smooth, soft, pliable ball that is slightly tacky to the touch.

3. After the baking cycle ends, remove bread from pan, place on cake rack, and allow to cool 1 hour before slicing.

CRUST: Light
BAKE CYCLE: Standard
OPTIONAL BAKE CYCLES: Sweet Bread / Rapid Bake

NUTRITIONAL INFORMATION PER SLICE
Calories 150 / Fat 3.6 grams / Carbohydrates 24.7 grams / Protein 4.2 grams / Fiber .8 gram / Sodium 273 milligrams / Cholesterol 31 milligrams

---

French Bread Extraordinaire!

*T*his method, though time-consuming, produces an exceptional loaf of French bread, much like the ones baked in the boulangeries of Paris. The extra risings fully develop the bread's flavor. The finished loaf will have a crisp crust and very moist, chewy interior. Bon appétit!

	SMALL	MEDIUM	LARGE
WATER	⅞ cup	1⅛ to 1¼ cups	1½ to 1⅝ cups
UNBLEACHED WHITE FLOUR	2⅓ cups	3½ cups	4⅔ cups
SALT	1 teaspoon	1½ teaspoons	2 teaspoons
RED STAR BRAND ACTIVE DRY YEAST	2 teaspoons	2 teaspoons	2½ teaspoons

1. Place dough ingredients in bread pan, select Dough setting, and press Start.

2. When the dough cycle ends, the machine will beep. Set a time and allow the dough to rise 1 more hour. Open the machine, punch down the dough, set the time again, and let dough rise another hour in the machine. Turn off bread machine, remove bread pan, and turn out dough onto a lightly floured countertop or cutting board. Form into a smooth, round ball then flatten it with your hands.

3. Place a clean kitchen towel (not terry cloth) in a round wicker basket that's at least twice the size of the dough. Dust the towel liberally with flour. Place the round dough in the center of the basket. Place basket in a warm place and let dough rise, uncovered, about 45 minutes until doubled in size.

4. Gently turn dough out of basket upside down onto a greased baking sheet. With a very sharp knife held almost parallel to the loaf, carefully slash the top of the dough at sharp angles in a # pattern.

5. Preheat oven to 450°F. Carefully place a small pan on the floor or bottom shelf of the oven. Add at least 1 cup boiling water to the pan. Place dough in oven and bake for 20 minutes. Remove from oven and place on cake rack to cool 1 hour before slicing. To preserve the crisp crust, do not store in plastic wrap or bag. Bread can be loosely covered or left out for up to 2 days before it dries out completely.

VARIATION:

If you want to make French breads with crusts so thin and crisp they crackle when you remove them from the oven, try baking this bread in a La Cloche clay cooker. They're sold in both round and oblong shapes in gourmet cooking stores, or check the Sources section (page 215) for supplier.

I. Omit steps 3 through 5, liberally cover base of La Cloche with cornmeal. Place the rounded dough onto the base.

2. Slash the dough as indicated in step 4. Cover it with a clean towel (again, not terry cloth), then place it in a warm oven to rise until doubled in size, about 30 to 45 minutes.

3. While the dough is rising, soak the lid of La Cloche upside down in a sink of water. (Cushion the handle with a dishcloth or sponge.)*

4. For a dark crust, preheat the oven to 450°F. Place the wet lid over the dough; bake for 30 minutes. Remove the lid and bake for another 10 to 15 minutes, until dark brown.

5. For a lighter crust, preheat the oven to 450°F. Place the wet lid over the dough; bake for 15 minutes. Reduce the heat to 400°F and bake for another 15 minutes. Remove the lid and bake for 8 to 10 minutes, until golden brown.

Yields 1 loaf

BAKE CYCLE: Dough

NUTRITIONAL INFORMATION PER SLICE
Calories 115 / Fat .3 grams / Carbohydrates 23.9 grams / Protein 3.4 grams / Fiber .9 grams / Sodium 230 milligrams / Cholesterol 0 milligrams

---

*The manufacturer of La Cloche, Sassafras Enterprises, does not recommend soaking the lid before baking because the absorption factor of stoneware is less than 1 percent. We call for soaking the lid in our recipe because we tested it both ways and preferred the crust of the bread baked with the soaked lid. A third option is to skip the soaking step but spritz the inside of the lid with a little water just before placing it over the dough.

Garlic Cheese Rolls

*T*hese garlicky rolls are incredibly light and delicious hot out of the oven! We've also found that they go over very well at potluck suppers.

	SMALL	MEDIUM	LARGE
DOUGH			
WATER	¾ cup	1 cup	1¼ cups
SALT	1 teaspoon	1½ teaspoons	2 teaspoons
BUTTER OR MARGARINE	1 tablespoon	1½ tablespoons	2 tablespoons
SUGAR	2 tablespoons	3 tablespoons	¼ cup
ALL-PURPOSE FLOUR	2 cups	3 cups	4 cups
NONFAT DRY MILK POWDER	1 tablespoon	2 tablespoons	2 tablespoons
RED STAR BRAND ACTIVE DRY YEAST	1½ teaspoons	1½ teaspoons	2 teaspoons
TOPPING			
MELTED BUTTER OR MARGARINE	¼ cup	¼ cup	½ cup
GARLIC CLOVE, CRUSHED	1	1	2
GRATED PARMESAN CHEESE	2 tablespoons	2 tablespoons	¼ cup

I. Place dough ingredients in bread pan, select Dough setting, and press Start.

2. When the dough has risen long enough, the machine will beep. Turn off bread machine, remove bread pan, and turn out dough onto a lightly floured countertop or cutting board. Gently roll and stretch dough into a 24-inch rope.

For the Small Recipe
Grease two 8-inch pie pans. With a sharp knife, divide dough into 16 pieces. (*Hint:* First cut dough into 8 equal pieces, then cut each of those in half.)

For the Medium Recipe
Grease two 8-inch pie pans. With a sharp knife, divide dough into 24 pieces. (*Hint:* First cut dough into 12 equal pieces, then cut each of those in half.)

For the Large Recipe

Grease three 8-inch pie pans. With a sharp knife, divide dough into 32 pieces. (*Hint:* First cut dough into 8 equal pieces, then cut each of those into 4 pieces.)

3. Shape each piece into a ball and place in prepared pie pans. In a small bowl, combine butter and garlic; pour over rolls. Sprinkle with Parmesan cheese.

4. Cover and let rise in a warm oven 30 to 45 minutes until doubled in size. (*Hint:* To warm oven slightly, turn oven on Warm setting for 1 minute, then turn it off, and place covered dough in oven to rise. Remove pan from oven before preheating.)

5. Preheat oven to 375°F. Bake for 15 minutes until golden. Remove from oven, cut apart, and serve warm.

Small recipe yields 16 rolls
Medium recipe yields 24 rolls
Large recipe yields 32 rolls

BAKE CYCLE: Dough

NUTRITIONAL INFORMATION PER ROLL
Calories 90 / Fat 2.9 grams / Carbohydrates 13.8 grams / Protein 2 grams / Fiber .5 gram / Sodium 174 milligrams / Cholesterol .4 milligram

---

Ham and Pepper Cheese Bread

Perk up your spirits and your taste buds some gloomy day with this spicy sand-wich loaf. It freezes well and can be microwaved for a quick lunch. If you pre-fer, use sliced turkey or roast beef instead of ham. Let your imagination be your guide with this one.

	SMALL	MEDIUM	LARGE
DOUGH			
MILK	⅜ cup	½ cup	¾ cup
WATER	¼ cup	⅜ cup	⅝ cup
EGG	1	1	2
OIL	1 tablespoon	1½ tablespoons	2 tablespoons
SALT	1 teaspoon	1½ teaspoons	2 teaspoons
SUGAR	2 tablespoons	3 tablespoons	¼ cup
BREAD FLOUR	2 cups	3 cups	4 cups
WHEAT GERM	2 tablespoons	3 tablespoons	¼ cup
INSTANT POTATO FLAKES	1 tablespoon	2 tablespoons	3 tablespoons
RED STAR BRAND ACTIVE DRY YEAST	1½ teaspoons	1½ teaspoons	2 teaspoons

FILLING			
THIN SLICES HAM	6	8	12
GRATED CHEDDAR CHEESE	1 cup (4 ounces)	1½ cups (6 ounces)	2 cups (8 ounces)
GRATED JALAPEÑO PEPPER CHEESE	1 cup (4 ounces)	1½ cups (6 ounces)	2 cups (8 ounces)

1. Place dough ingredients in bread pan, select Dough setting, and press Start.

2. When the dough has risen long enough, the machine will beep. Turn off bread machine, remove bread pan, and turn out dough onto a lightly floured countertop or cutting board.

For the Small Recipe

With a rolling pin, roll dough into a 10x15-inch rectangle.

For the Medium Recipe

With a rolling pin, roll dough into a 12x21-inch rectangle.

For the Large Recipe

With a sharp knife, divide dough in half. With a rolling pin, roll dough into two 10x15-inch rectangles.

3. Grease one or two large baking sheets. Preheat oven to 350°F.

4. Cover dough with ham and sprinkle cheeses on top. Starting at long edge, roll up tightly; pinch seam and ends to seal. Place seam-side down on prepared baking sheet.

5. Bake for 30 minutes until brown. Remove from oven and allow to cool for 2 minutes. Slice into 3-inch-wide pieces. Serve warm.

Small recipe yields 5 sandwiches
Medium recipe yields 7 sandwiches
Large recipe yields 10 sandwiches

BAKE CYCLE: Dough

NUTRITIONAL INFORMATION PER SLICE
Calories 507 / Fat 21.7 grams / Carbohydrates 50.1 grams / Protein 26.4 grams / Fiber 2.1 grams / Sodium 1220 milligrams / Cholesterol 93.3 milligrams

---

Heavenly Whole Wheat Bread

W*e think this is the best of our whole wheat breads. It's moist, has a good crust, and has a flavor that's out of this world.*

	SMALL	MEDIUM	LARGE
WATER	¾ to ⅞ cup	1⅛ to 1¼ cups	1⅝ to 1¾ cups
SALT	1 teaspoon	1¼ teaspoons	2 teaspoons
BUTTER OR MARGARINE	3 tablespoons	4 tablespoons	6 tablespoons
SUGAR	1 tablespoon	2 tablespoons	2 tablespoons
WHOLE WHEAT FLOUR	1⅓ cups	2 cups	2⅔ cups
BREAD FLOUR	⅔ cup	1 cup	1⅓ cups
INSTANT POTATO FLAKES	3 tablespoons	¼ cup	6 tablespoons
VITAL WHEAT GLUTEN, OPTIONAL	2 tablespoons	3 tablespoons to ⅓ cup	4 tablespoons
RED STAR BRAND ACTIVE DRY YEAST	1½ teaspoons	2 teaspoons	2 teaspoons

1. Place all ingredients in bread pan, using the least amount of liquid listed in the recipe. Select Medium Crust setting and Whole Wheat cycle. Press Start.

2. Observe the dough as it kneads. After 5 to 10 minutes, if it appears dry and stiff or if your machine sounds as if it's straining to knead it, add more liquid 1 tablespoon at a time until dough forms a smooth, soft, pliable ball that is slightly tacky to the touch.

3. After the baking cycle ends, remove bread from pan, place on cake rack, and allow to cool 1 hour before slicing.

CRUST: Medium

BAKE CYCLE: Whole Wheat

OPTIONAL BAKE CYCLES: Standard / Sweet Bread / Delayed Timer / Rapid Bake

---

NUTRITIONAL INFORMATION PER SLICE
Calories 130 / Fat 3.7 grams / Carbohydrates 21.7 grams / Protein 3.5 grams / Fiber 2.5 grams / Sodium 269 milligrams / Cholesterol 0 milligram

---

Herb Bread

Plan to be around while this one bakes, because the aroma is absolutely out of this world! As for the taste, it's hard to limit yourself to just one slice of this zesty bread. We recommend it for croutons, also. (Note: When making the small loaf, use the Rapid Bake setting for a better-shaped bread.)

	SMALL	MEDIUM	LARGE
MILK	¾ to ⅞ cup	⅞ to 1 cup	1½ to 1⅝ cups
SALT	1 teaspoon	1½ teaspoons	1½ teaspoons
SUGAR	1 tablespoon	1½ tablespoons	2 tablespoons
BUTTER OR MARGARINE	2 tablespoons	3 tablespoons	¼ cup
CHOPPED ONION	⅓ cup	½ cup	⅔ cup
BREAD FLOUR	2 cups	3 cups	4 cups
DRIED DILL	½ teaspoon	½ teaspoon	1 teaspoon
DRIED BASIL	½ teaspoon	½ teaspoon	1 teaspoon
DRIED ROSEMARY	½ teaspoon	½ teaspoon	1 teaspoon
RED STAR BRAND ACTIVE DRY YEAST	1½ teaspoons	2 teaspoons	2½ teaspoons

For the Small Recipe

I. Place all ingredients in bread pan, using the least amount of liquid listed in the recipe. Select Medium Crust setting, the Rapid Bake cycle, and press Start.

2. Observe the dough as it kneads. After 5 to 10 minutes, if it appears dry and stiff or if your machine sounds as if it's straining to knead it, add more liquid 1 tablespoon at a time until dough forms a smooth, soft, pliable ball that is slightly tacky to the touch.

3. After the baking cycle ends, remove bread from pan, place on cake rack, and allow to cool 1 hour before slicing.

CRUST: Medium
BAKE CYCLE: Rapid Bake

For the Medium and Large Recipes

1. Place all ingredients in bread pan, using the least amount of liquid listed in the recipe. Select Light Crust setting and press Start.

2. Observe the dough as it kneads. After 5 to 10 minutes, if it appears dry and stiff or if your machine sounds as if it's straining to knead it, add more liquid 1 tablespoon at a time until dough forms a smooth, soft, pliable ball that is slightly tacky to the touch.

3. After the baking cycle ends, remove bread from pan, place on cake rack, and allow to cool 1 hour before slicing.

CRUST: Light
BAKE CYCLE: Standard

NUTRITIONAL INFORMATION PER SLICE
Calories 138 / Fat 3.3 grams / Carbohydrates 23.2 grams / Protein 3.5 grams / Fiber .9 gram / Sodium 259 milligrams / Cholesterol 9 milligrams

---

Herb Rolls

*S*uch *excellent rolls deserve a fine dinner. They go well with everything from prime roast beef to homemade chicken soup. (*Note: *If you make these ahead of time, cover to prevent them from turning hard.)*

	SMALL	MEDIUM	LARGE
BUTTER OR MARGARINE	3 tablespoons	4 tablespoons	5 tablespoons
FINELY CHOPPED ONION	2 tablespoons	3 tablespoons	¼ cup
GARLIC CLOVE(S), MINCED	1 medium	1 large	2 medium
DRIED OREGANO	½ teaspoon	¾ teaspoon	1 teaspoon
DRIED BASIL	½ teaspoon	¾ teaspoon	1 teaspoon
DRIED TARRAGON	½ teaspoon	¾ teaspoon	1 teaspoon
WATER	¾ cup	1 cup	1⅜ cups
SALT	1 teaspoon	1 teaspoon	1½ teaspoons
SUGAR	1 teaspoon	1½ teaspoons	2 teaspoons
ALL-PURPOSE FLOUR	2 cups	3 cups	4 cups
RED STAR BRAND ACTIVE DRY YEAST	1½ teaspoons	1½ teaspoons	2 teaspoons

I. In a small skillet, melt the butter. Add onion, garlic, and herbs. Sauté over medium heat until onion is soft, about 5 minutes. Cool to room temperature.

2. Place all ingredients, including onion mixture, in bread pan, select Dough setting, and press Start.

3. When the dough has risen long enough, the machine will beep. Turn off bread machine, remove bread pan, and turn out dough onto a lightly floured countertop or cutting board.

4. Gently roll and stretch dough into an 18-inch rope.

For the Small Recipe

Grease a 12-cup muffin tin, a 9x13x2-inch pan, or baking sheet. With a sharp knife, divide dough into 12 pieces.

For the Medium Recipe

Grease a 12-cup muffin tin, 9x13x2-inch pan, or large baking sheet. With a sharp knife, divide dough into 18 pieces. (*Hint:* First cut dough into 6 equal pieces, then cut each of those into 3 pieces.)

For the Large Recipe

Grease two 12-cup muffin tins, two 9x13x2-inch pans, or two baking sheets. With a sharp knife, divide dough into 24 pieces. (*Hint:* First cut dough into 6 equal pieces, then cut each of those into 4 pieces.)

5. Roll dough into balls: place in prepared pan(s). Cover and let rise in a warm oven 30 to 45 minutes until doubled. (*Hint:* To warm oven slightly, turn oven on Warm setting for 1 minute, then turn it off, and place covered dough in oven to rise. Remove from oven to preheat.)

6. Preheat oven to 400°F. Bake for 12 to 15 minutes until golden brown. Remove from oven and serve warm.

Small recipe yields 12 rolls
Medium recipe yields 18 rolls
Large recipe yields 24 rolls

BAKE CYCLE: Dough

NUTRITIONAL INFORMATION PER ROLL
Calories 102 / Fat 2.8 grams / Carbohydrates 16.5 grams / Protein 2.3 grams / Fiber .7 grams / Sodium 141 milligrams / Cholesterol 6.9 milligrams

---

Honey Wheat Rolls

*T*hese dinner rolls are far superior to any packaged rolls you can buy. They're lovely on the Thanksgiving table and also very popular as a snack fresh out of the oven, split in half, and filled with thinly sliced ham and a dab of mustard. Either way, they disappear in a hurry!

	SMALL	MEDIUM	LARGE
WATER	½ cup	¾ cup	⅞ cup
EGG	1	1	2
HONEY	1½ tablespoons	2 tablespoons	3 tablespoons
SALT	½ teaspoon	1 teaspoon	1½ teaspoons
BUTTER OR MARGARINE	1½ tablespoons	2 tablespoons	3 tablespoons
ALL-PURPOSE FLOUR	1⅓ cups	2 cups	2⅔ cups
WHOLE WHEAT FLOUR	⅔ cup	1 cup	1⅓ cups
RED STAR BRAND ACTIVE DRY YEAST	1½ teaspoons	1½ teaspoons	2 teaspoons

1. Place dough ingredients in bread pan, select Dough setting, and press Start.

2. When the dough has risen long enough, the machine will beep. Turn off bread machine, remove bread pan, and turn out dough onto a lightly floured countertop or cutting board. Gently roll and stretch dough into an 18-inch rope.

For the Small Recipe
Grease one 12-cup muffin tin. With a sharp knife, divide dough into 12 pieces.

For the Medium Recipe
Grease two 12-cup muffin tins. With a sharp knife, divide dough into 18 pieces. (*Hint:* First cut dough into 6 equal pieces, then cut each of those into 3 pieces.)

For the Large Recipe
Grease two 12-cup muffin tins. With a sharp knife, divide dough into 24 pieces. (*Hint:* First cut dough into 12 equal pieces, then cut each of those in half.)

3. Place rolls in muffin tin(s). Cover and let rise in a warm oven 20 to 30 minutes until doubled in size. (*Hint:* To warm oven slightly, turn oven on Warm setting for 1

minute, then turn it off, and place covered dough in oven to rise. Remove pan from oven before preheating.)

4. Preheat oven to 400°F. Bake for 12 minutes until brown. Remove from oven and serve warm.

Small recipe yields 12 rolls
Medium recipe yields 18 rolls
Large recipe yields 24 rolls

BAKE CYCLE: Dough

NUTRITIONAL INFORMATION PER ROLL
Calories 96 / Fat 1.8 grams / Carbohydrates 17.4 grams / Protein 2.8 grams / Fiber 1.3 grams / Sodium 138 milligrams / Cholesterol 11.8 milligrams

---

Honey 'n' Oats Bread

The egg and oats lend a wonderful rich, creamy flavor to this bread. Serve it with a crock of sweet butter and homemade preserves.

	SMALL	MEDIUM	LARGE
OLD-FASHIONED ROLLED OATS	⅓ cup	½ cup	⅔ cup
BUTTERMILK	¾ to ⅞ cup	1 to 1⅛ cups	1⅜ to 1½ cups
EGG	1	1	2
HONEY	1 tablespoon	1½ tablespoons	2 tablespoons
SALT	1 teaspoon	1½ teaspoons	2 teaspoons
WHOLE WHEAT FLOUR	1 cup	1½ cups	2 cups
BREAD FLOUR	1 cup	1½ cups	2 cups
VITAL WHEAT GLUTEN, OPTIONAL	1½ tablespoons	2 tablespoons	3 tablespoons
RED STAR BRAND ACTIVE DRY YEAST	1½ teaspoons	2 teaspoons	2½ teaspoons

1. Place all ingredients in bread pan, using the least amount of liquid listed in the recipe. Select Medium Crust setting and Whole Wheat cycle. Press Start.

2. Observe the dough as it kneads. After 5 to 10 minutes, if it appears dry and stiff or if your machine sounds as if it's straining to knead it, add more liquid 1 tablespoon at a time until dough forms a smooth, soft, pliable ball that is slightly tacky to the touch.

3. After the baking cycle ends, remove bread from pan, place on cake rack, and allow to cool 1 hour before slicing.

CRUST: Medium
BAKE CYCLE: Whole Wheat
OPTIONAL BAKE CYCLES: Standard / Sweet Bread / Rapid Bake

NUTRITIONAL INFORMATION PER SLICE
Calories 124 / Fat 1.1 grams / Carbohydrates 24.2 grams / Protein 4.8 grams / Fiber 2.4 grams / Sodium 252 milligrams / Cholesterol 15.9 milligrams

---

Irene's Bavarian Coffee Cake

*O*ur friend Irene thought this was the best of all the breads and coffee cakes we asked our co-workers to taste-test while devising recipes for this book. Once you make it, you'll understand why. Not only is this coffee cake very velvety rich and spicy, it is amazingly quick and easy to create. We think it could be served for dessert following a light meal.

	SMALL	MEDIUM	LARGE
DOUGH			
MILK	¼ cup	⅜ cup	¼ cup
WATER	¼ cup	⅜ cup	¼ cup
EGG	1	1	2
SALT	1 teaspoon	1 teaspoon	2 teaspoons
BUTTER OR MARGARINE	3 tablespoons	4 tablespoons	6 tablespoons
SUGAR	¼ cup	⅓ cup	½ cup
ALL-PURPOSE FLOUR	2 cups	3 cups	4 cups
RED STAR BRAND ACTIVE DRY YEAST	1½ teaspoons	1½ teaspoons	2 teaspoons
TOPPING			
SUGAR	¼ cup	⅓ cup	½ cup
GROUND CINNAMON	¾ teaspoon	1 teaspoon	1½ teaspoons
HEAVY CREAM	⅔ cup	1 cup	1⅓ cups

1. Place dough ingredients in bread pan, select Dough setting, and press Start.

2. When the dough has risen long enough, the machine will beep. Turn off bread machine, remove bread pan, and turn out dough onto a lightly floured countertop or cutting board.

For the Small Recipe

Grease a 9-inch round or square cake pan. With a rolling pin, roll dough into a 9-inch square or circle, depending on the pan you are using.

For the Medium Recipe

Grease a 9x13x2-inch pan. With a rolling pin, roll dough into a 9x13-inch rectangle.

For the Large Recipe

Grease two 9-inch round or square cake pans. With a sharp knife, divide dough in half. With a rolling pin, roll dough into a 9-inch square or circle, depending on the pan you are using.

3. Place dough in prepared pan. Cover and let rise in a warm oven 45 to 60 minutes until doubled in size. (*Hint:* To warm oven slightly, turn oven on Warm setting for 1 minute, then turn it off, and place covered dough in oven to rise. Remove pan from oven before preheating.)

4. With 2 fingers, punch deep holes all over the dough. In a small bowl, combine sugar and cinnamon; sprinkle mixture over dough. Drizzle cream evenly on top.

5. Preheat oven to 350°F. Bake for 25 to 30 minutes until a tester inserted in the middle of the cake comes out clean. Remove from oven and serve warm.

Small recipe yields one 9-inch round or square coffee cake
Medium recipe yields one 9x13-inch coffee cake
Large recipe yields two 9-inch round or square coffee cakes

BAKE CYCLE: Dough

NUTRITIONAL INFORMATION PER SERVING
Calories 216 / Fat 9.6 grams / Carbohydrates 28.9 grams / Protein 3.7 grams / Fiber .8 gram / Sodium 192 milligrams / Cholesterol 36.2 milligrams

---

Jalapeño Cheese Bread

Wow—hot stuff! Serve this coarsely textured, very spicy bread at your next cocktail party and watch it disappear. It's great with a glass of wine or a cold beer, but its perfect partner is a frosty margarita!

	SMALL	MEDIUM	LARGE
SOUR CREAM	½ cup	¾ cup	¾ cup
WATER	⅛ to ¼ cup	⅛ to ¼ cup	⅝ to ¾ cup
EGG	1	1	2
SALT	1 teaspoon	1½ teaspoons	2 teaspoons
SUGAR	1½ tablespoons	2 tablespoons	3 tablespoons
BREAD FLOUR	2 cups	3 cups	4 cups
GRATED SHARP CHEDDAR CHEESE	¾ cup (3 ounces)	1 cup (4 ounces)	1 cup (4 ounces)
SEEDED AND CHOPPED FRESH JALAPEÑO PEPPER OR CANNED DICED JALAPEÑO PEPPERS	2 tablespoons (about 3 peppers)	3 tablespoons (about 4 peppers)	¼ cup (5 to 6 peppers)
RED STAR BRAND ACTIVE DRY YEAST	1½ teaspoons	2 teaspoons	2½ teaspoons

1. Place all ingredients in bread pan, using the least amount of liquid listed in the recipe. Select Light Crust setting and press Start.

2. Observe the dough as it kneads. After 5 to 10 minutes, if it appears dry and stiff or if your machine sounds as if it's straining to knead it, add more liquid 1 tablespoon at a time until dough forms a smooth, soft, pliable ball that is slightly tacky to the touch.

3. After the baking cycle ends, remove bread from pan, place on cake rack, and allow to cool 1 hour before slicing.

CRUST: Light
BAKE CYCLE: Standard
OPTIONAL BAKE CYCLES: Whole Wheat / Sweet Bread / Raisin Nut

NUTRITIONAL INFORMATION PER SLICE
Calories 169 / Fat 5.9 grams / Carbohydrates 23 grams / Protein 5.7 grams / Fiber .9 grams /
Sodium 305 milligrams / Cholesterol 29.2 milligrams

Jana's Seed and Nut Bread

W*e shared this glorious loaf with the staff of J.C.'s Kitchen Company in San Diego, people with very discriminating taste buds. To our delight, it earned a unanimous thumbs-up! So we thought it fitting to name it in honor of the store's owner, Jana Cason. Jana suggests serving it with a flavored cream-cheese spread. (Note: We had some problems with this loaf overflowing in the 1-pound machines occasionally. We recommend you keep an eye on it the first time you try it.)*

	SMALL	MEDIUM	LARGE
WATER	⅝ cup	⅞ t 1 cup	1 to 1⅛ cups
EGG	1	1	2
OIL	2 tablespoons	2 tablespoons	¼ cup
SALT	1½ teaspoons	2 teaspoons	2 teaspoons
BROWN SUGAR	3 tablespoons	¼ cup	6 tablespoons
BREAD FLOUR	2¼ cups	3 cups	4½ cups
CHOPPED, TOASTED PECANS*	½ cup	1 cup	1 cup
RAW, UNSALTED SUNFLOWER SEEDS, TOASTED*	2 tablespoons	¼ cup	¼ cup
CHOPPED, TOASTED WALNUTS*	2 tablespoons	¼ cup	¼ cup
RED STAR BRAND ACTIVE DRY YEAST	1½ teaspoons	2 teaspoons	2½ teaspoons

1. Place all ingredients in bread pan, using the least amount of liquid listed in the recipe. Select Light Crust setting and press Start.

2. Observe the dough as it kneads. After 5 to 10 minutes, if it appears dry and stiff or if your machine sounds as if it's straining to knead it, add more liquid 1 tablespoon at a time until dough forms a smooth, soft, pliable ball that is slightly tacky to the touch.

*To toast pecans, walnuts, and sunflower seeds, place them in a small pan and bake in a 350°F oven for 8 to 10 minutes.

3. After the baking cycle ends, remove bread from pan, place on cake rack, and allow to cool 1 hour before slicing.

CRUST: Medium

BAKE CYCLE: Standard

OPTIONAL BAKE CYCLES: Sweet Bread / Rapid Bake / Raisin Nut

NUTRITIONAL INFORMATION PER SLICE

Calories 221 / Fat 10.9 grams / Carbohydrates 26.7 grams / Protein 4.9 grams / Fiber 1.7 grams / Sodium 312 milligrams / Cholesterol 15.2 milligrams

---

Jim's Cinnamon Rolls

Nothing can top the aroma and warm, sweet stickiness of cinnamon rolls, fresh from the oven. What you'll also love about these luscious, light rolls is that the machine does half the work; they're no longer a major production. The first time Lois made these, her husband Jim emphatically declared them his favorite recipe of all—high praise from one who had been completely noncommittal about the breads until then!

	SMALL	MEDIUM	LARGE
DOUGH			
MILK	¼ cup	⅜ cup	⅜ cup
WATER	¼ cup	⅜ cup	⅜ cup
EGG	1	1	2
SALT	1 teaspoon	1 teaspoon	2 teaspoons
BUTTER OR MARGARINE	3 tablespoons	4 tablespoons	6 tablespoons
SUGAR	¼ cup	⅓ cup	½ cup
ALL-PURPOSE FLOUR	2 cups	3 cups	4 cups
RED STAR BRAND ACTIVE DRY YEAST	1½ teaspoons	1½ teaspoons	2 teaspoons
GLAZE			
MELTED BUTTER OR MARGARINE	3 tablespoons	5 tablespoons	6 tablespoons
BROWN SUGAR	⅓ cup	½ cup	⅔ cup
FILLING			
MELTED BUTTER OR MARGARINE	1 tablespoon	1 tablespoon	2 tablespoons
GRANULATED SUGAR	1 tablespoon	2 tablespoons	2 tablespoons
GROUND CINNAMON	1½ teaspoons	1 tablespoon	1 tablespoon
BROWN SUGAR	1 tablespoon	2 tablespoons	2 tablespoons
RAISINS, OPTIONAL	⅓ cup	½ cup	⅔ cup

1. Place dough ingredients in bread pan, select Dough setting, and press Start.

2. When the dough has risen long enough, the machine will beep. Turn off bread machine, remove bread pan, and turn out dough onto a lightly floured countertop or cutting board.

For the Small Recipe

Pour the melted butter for the glaze into one 9-inch round or square cake pan; sprinkle with brown sugar. With a rolling pin, roll dough into an 8x14-inch rectangle.

For the Medium Recipe

Pour the melted butter for the glaze into one 9x13x2-inch pan or two 8- or 9-inch round or square cake pans; sprinkle with brown sugar. With a rolling pin, roll dough into a 9x18-inch rectangle.

For the Large Recipe

Pour the melted butter for the glaze into two 9-inch round or square cake pans; sprinkle with brown sugar. Divide dough in half. With a rolling pin, roll each ball of dough into an 8x14-inch rectangle.

For the Filling

3. Brush the melted butter on the dough. In a small bowl, combine the granulated sugar, cinnamon, brown sugar, and raisins; sprinkle over dough. Starting with long edge, roll up dough; pinch seams to seal. With a knife, lightly mark roll into 1½-inch sections. Slide a 12-inch piece of dental floss or heavy thread underneath. By bringing the ends of the floss up and crisscrossing them at the top of each mark, you can cut through the roll by pulling the strings in opposite directions. Place rolls cut side up in prepared pan(s), flattening them slightly.* Cover and let rise in a warm oven 30 to 45 minutes until doubled. (*Hint:* To warm oven slightly, turn oven on Warm setting for 1 minute, then turn it off, and place covered dough in oven to rise. Remove pan(s) from oven to preheat.)

4. Preheat oven to 350°F. Bake for 25 to 30 minutes until golden brown. Remove from oven and immediately invert rolls onto a large platter or serving dish. Serve warm.

---

*The rolls can be covered with foil at this point and refrigerated overnight or frozen for 1 month. Before baking, allow rolls to thaw completely and rise in a warm oven for at least 30 minutes.

Small recipe yields 9 rolls
Medium recipe yields 12 rolls
Large recipe yields 18 rolls

BAKE CYCLE: Dough

NUTRITIONAL INFORMATION PER ROLL

Calories 302 / Fat 10.6 grams / Carbohydrates 48.1 grams / Protein 4.4 grams / Fiber 1.4 grams / Sodium 274 milligrams / Cholesterol 44.7 milligrams

---

Jim's Maple Walnut Bread

*J*im *Bodle of Clockville, New York, sent us this recipe. He loves just about anything that has maple syrup in it, so once he purchased his bread machine, he decided to create a maple syrup bread. We're certainly glad he did! This bread was a huge hit when shared with friends.*

	SMALL	MEDIUM	LARGE
WATER	⅝ to ¾ cup	⅞ to 1 cup	1⅛ to 1¼ cups
MAPLE SYRUP	¼ cup	½ cup	½ cup
SALT	¾ teaspoon	1 teaspoon	1½ teaspoons
BUTTER OR MARGARINE	2 teaspoons	1 tablespoon	4 teaspoons
SUGAR	2 teaspoons	1 tablespoon	4 teaspoons
BREAD FLOUR	2 cups	3 cups	4 cups
NONFAT DRY MILK POWDER	1½ tablespoons	2 tablespoons	3 tablespoons
WALNUTS, CHOPPED	3 tablespoons	¼ cup	6 tablespoons
RED STAR BRAND ACTIVE DRY YEAST	1½ teaspoons	2 teaspoons	2½ teaspoons

1. Place all ingredients in bread pan, using the least amount of liquid listed in the recipe. Select Light Crust setting and press Start.

2. Observe the dough as it kneads. After 5 to 10 minutes, if it appears dry and stiff or if your machine sounds as if it's straining to knead it, add more liquid 1 tablespoon at a time until dough forms a smooth, soft, pliable ball that is slightly tacky to the touch.

3. After the baking cycle ends, remove bread from pan, place on cake rack, and allow to cool 1 hour before slicing.

CRUST: Light
BAKE CYCLE: Standard
OPTIONAL BAKE CYCLES: Whole Wheat / Sweet Bread / Raisin Nut / Delayed Timer / Rapid Bake

---

NUTRITIONAL INFORMATION PER SLICE
Calories 153 / Fat 2.4 grams / Carbohydrates 29.5 grams / Protein 3.4 grams / Fiber .9 grams / Sodium 165 milligrams / Cholesterol 2.3 milligrams

---

L & L Bakers' Dill Bread

A mong the many virtues of this bread are its pungent herb and onion flavor and its very light texture. In addition, it holds a special significance for us. It was such a big hit as a gift that it eventually became the starting point of our first cookbook, Bread Machine Magic. *We urge you to give this as a gift and see what good fortune awaits you, too.*

	SMALL	MEDIUM	LARGE
MILK	3 tablespoons	¼ cup	6 tablespoons
WATER	3 to 4 tablespoons	¼ to ⅜ cup	6 to 8 tablespoons
EGG	1	1	2
SALT	1 teaspoon	1½ teaspoons	2 teaspoons
BUTTER OR MARGARINE	1 tablespoon	1½ tablespoons	2 tablespoons
SUGAR	2 tablespoons	3 tablespoons	¼ cup
LOW-FAT COTTAGE CHEESE	⅓ cup	⅔ cup	⅔ cup
BREAD FLOUR	2 cups	3 cups	4 cups
DRIED MINCED ONION	1 tablespoon	2 tablespoons	2 tablespoons
DRIED DILL WEED	2 teaspoons	1 tablespoon	4 teaspoons
DRIED PARSLEY FLAKES	2 teaspoons	1 tablespoon	4 teaspoons
RED STAR BRAND ACTIVE DRY YEAST	1½ teaspoons	2 teaspoons	2½ teaspoons

1. Place all ingredients in bread pan, using the least amount of liquid listed in the recipe. Select Light Crust setting and press Start.

2. Observe the dough as it kneads. After 5 to 10 minutes, if it appears dry and stiff or if your machine sounds as if it's straining to knead it, add more liquid 1 tablespoon at a time until dough forms a smooth, soft, pliable ball that is slightly tacky to the touch.

3. After the baking cycle ends, remove bread from pan, place on cake rack, and allow to cool 1 hour before slicing.

CRUST: Light

BAKE CYCLE: Standard

OPTIONAL BAKE CYCLES: Sweet Bread / Rapid Bake

NUTRITIONAL INFORMATION PER SLICE

Calories 137 / Fat 2 grams / Carbohydrates 24.2 grams / Protein 4.9 grams / Fiber .9 grams / Sodium 294 milligrams / Cholesterol 15.9 milligrams

Linda's Lemon Bread

This sweet/sour, moist bread has a bright fresh taste and smells marvelous even when it's kneading. We love to have friends in for dessert and put small slices of this bread out on a pretty plate along with some leftover lemon curd.

	SMALL	MEDIUM	LARGE
OLD-FASHIONED ROLLED OATS	½ cup	⅔ cup	1 cup
MILK	⅞ to 1 cup	1⅛ to 1⅜ cups	1⅞ to 2 cups
LEMON CURD (RECIPE PAGE 183)	⅓ cup	½ cup	1 cup
SALT	1 teaspoon	1½ teaspoons	2 teaspoons
BUTTER OR MARGARINE	1 tablespoon	1½ tablespoons	2 tablespoons
BREAD FLOUR	2⅛ cups	3 cups	4¼ cups
RED STAR BRAND ACTIVE DRY YEAST	1½ teaspoons	2 teaspoons	2½ teaspoons

I. Place all ingredients in bread pan, using the least amount of liquid listed in the recipe. Select Light Crust setting and press Start.

2. Observe the recipe as it kneads. After 5 to 10 minutes, if it appears dry and stiff or if your machine sounds as if it's straining to knead it, add more liquid 1 tablespoon at a time until dough forms a smooth, soft, pliable ball that is slightly tacky to the touch.

3. After the baking cycle ends, remove bread from pan, place on cake rack, and allow to cool 1 hour before slicing.

CRUST: Light
BAKE CYCLE: Standard
OPTIONAL BAKE CYCLES: Sweet Bread / Rapid Bake

NUTRITIONAL INFORMATION PER SLICE
Calories 174 / Fat 3.4 grams / Carbohydrates 31.9 grams / Protein 4.2 grams / Fiber 1.4 grams / Sodium 252 milligrams / Cholesterol 6 milligrams

Lois's Country Crunch Bread

T his chewy loaf is Lois's favorite. When she tried it for the first time, she ex-
claimed, "Now this is what bread should taste like!" (Note: In the Zojirushi,
we had better results when we baked it on the Regular cycle rather than the French
Bread cycle.)

	SMALL	MEDIUM	LARGE
WATER	⅞ to 1 cup	1⅛ to 1¼ cups	1⅝ to 1¾ cups
SALT	1 teaspoon	1½ teaspoons	2 teaspoons
BUTTER OR MARGARINE	1 teaspoon	½ tablespoon	2 teaspoons
SUGAR	1 teaspoon	1½ teaspoons	2 teaspoons
BREAD FLOUR	2 cups	3 cups	4 cups
RED STAR BRAND ACTIVE DRY YEAST	1½ teaspoons	2 teaspoons	2½ teaspoons

I. Place all ingredients in bread pan, using the least amount of liquid listed in the
recipe. Select Medium Crust setting and press Start.

2. Observe the dough as it kneads. After 5 to 10 minutes, if it appears dry and stiff or
if your machine sounds as if it's straining to knead it, add more liquid 1 tablespoon

at a time until dough forms a smooth, soft, pliable ball that is slightly tacky to the touch.

3. After the baking cycle ends, remove bread from pan, place on cake rack, and allow to cool 1 hour before slicing.

CRUST: Medium
BAKE CYCLE: Standard
OPTIONAL BAKE CYCLES: French Bread / Delayed Timer / Rapid Bake

VARIATION:

1. Place dough ingredients in bread pan, select Dough setting, and press Start.

2. When the dough has risen long enough, the machine will beep. Turn off bread machine, remove bread pan, and turn out dough onto a lightly floured countertop or cutting board. Shape dough into a 15-inch log. Sprinkle a cookie sheet with cornmeal. Place dough on cookie sheet and brush with some olive oil. Cover with plastic wrap and refrigerate overnight.

3. Remove from refrigerator, uncover, let stand at room temperature one hour. Make 3 diagonal cuts with a sharp knife.

4. Preheat oven to 425°F. Bake 25 to 30 minutes until golden brown. Remove from oven and cool on cake rack.

BAKE CYCLE: Dough

NUTRITIONAL INFORMATION PER SLICE
Calories 104 / Fat .7 grams / Carbohydrates 20.9 grams / Protein 2.9 grams / Fiber .8 grams / Sodium 233 milligrams / Cholesterol 1.1 milligrams

---

Lorraine's Buttermilk Rye Bread

A good friend, and our favorite critic, Lorraine loved every loaf she sampled. She selected this as one of her favorites. We agree. With its creamy texture and rich flavor, it's perfect for sandwiches.

	SMALL	MEDIUM	LARGE
BUTTERMILK	⅞ to 1 cup	1⅜ to 1½ cups + 1 tablespoon	1⅞ to 2 cups
SALT	1 teaspoon	1½ teaspoons	2 teaspoons
BUTTER OR MARGARINE	1 tablespoon	1½ tablespoons	2 tablespoons
BROWN SUGAR	1½ tablespoons	2 tablespoons	3 tablespoons
BREAD FLOUR	2 cups	3 cups	4 cups
RYE FLOUR	⅓ cup	1 cup	⅔ cup
CARAWAY SEEDS	1 teaspoon	1 teaspoon	2 teaspoons
RED STAR BRAND ACTIVE DRY YEAST	2 teaspoons	3 teaspoons	3 teaspoons

1. Place all ingredients in bread pan, using the least amount of liquid listed in the recipe. Select Medium Crust setting and press Start.

2. Observe the dough as it kneads. After 5 to 10 minutes, if it appears dry and stiff or if your machine sounds as if it's straining to knead it, add more liquid 1 tablespoon at a time until dough forms a smooth, soft, pliable ball that is slightly tacky to the touch.

3. After the baking cycle ends, remove bread from pan, place on cake rack, and allow to cool 1 hour before slicing.

CRUST: Medium

BAKE CYCLE: Standard

OPTIONAL BAKE CYCLES: Whole Wheat / Sweet Bread

NUTRITIONAL INFORMATION PER SLICE
Calories 154 / Fat 1.9 grams / Carbohydrates 29.2 grams / Protein 4.5 grams / Fiber 2 grams / Sodium 270 milligrams / Cholesterol .9 milligrams

---

Marmalade and Oats Bread

Here's another winner. It's a beautiful-looking loaf, and the combination of orange marmalade and oatmeal makes it very tender, moist, and rich-tasting.

	SMALL	MEDIUM	LARGE
OLD-FASHIONED ROLLED OATS	½ cup	⅔ cup	1 cup
MILK	⅞ to 1 cup	1⅛ to 1¼ cups	1⅜ to 1½ cups
ORANGE MARMALADE	⅓ cup	½ cup	⅔ cup
BUTTER OR MARGARINE	1 tablespoon	1½ tablespoons	2 tablespoons
SALT	1 teaspoon	1½ teaspoons	2 teaspoons
BREAD FLOUR	2 cups	3 cups	4 cups
RED STAR BRAND ACTIVE DRY YEAST	1½ teaspoons	2 teaspoons	2 teaspoons

1. Place all ingredients in bread pan, using the least amount of liquid listed in the recipe. Select Medium Crust setting and press Start.

2. Observe the dough as it kneads. After 5 to 10 minutes, if it appears dry and stiff or if your machine sounds as if it's straining to knead it, add more liquid 1 tablespoon at a time until dough forms a smooth, soft, pliable ball that is slightly tacky to the touch.

3. After the baking cycle ends, remove bread from pan, place on cake rack, and allow to cool 1 hour before slicing.

CRUST: Medium
BAKE CYCLE: Standard
OPTIONAL BAKE CYCLES: Whole Wheat / Sweet Bread

NUTRITIONAL INFORMATION PER SLICE
Calories 162 / Fat 1.9 grams / Carbohydrates 31.9 grams / Protein 4.2 grams / Fiber 1.3 grams / Sodium 256 milligrams / Cholesterol .8 milligrams

---

Max's Clogging Bread

A *good friend brought us this recipe and we adapted it for the bread machine. Now the book just wouldn't be complete without it. Share a bottle of wine and a loaf of this aromatic bread with friends and soon everyone will feel like clogging the taps right off their shoes, just like our friend Max!*

DOUGH

	SMALL	MEDIUM	LARGE
WATER	¾ cup	1 cup	1¼ cup
SALT	1 teaspoon	1½ teaspoons	2 teaspoons
SUGAR	2 teaspoons	1 tablespoon	4 teaspoons
ALL-PURPOSE FLOUR	2 cups	3 cups	4 cups
FINELY CHOPPED ONION	¼ cup	⅓ cup	½ cup
RED STAR BRAND ACTIVE DRY YEAST	2 teaspoons	2 teaspoons	2½ teaspoons

TOPPING

OLIVE OIL	To taste	To taste	To taste
COARSE KOSHER SALT	To taste	To taste	To taste
DRIED ROSEMARY	To taste	To taste	To taste

1. Place dough ingredients in bread pan, select Dough setting, and press Start.

2. When the dough has risen long enough, the machine will beep. Turn off bread machine, remove bread pan, and turn out dough onto a lightly floured countertop or cutting board.

3. Oil a baking sheet with olive oil. Preheat oven to 400°F.

4. Rub some olive oil onto your hands. Place dough on oiled sheet and, with oiled hands, flatten it into a 1-inch thick circle or oblong shape. Sprinkle with salt and rosemary to taste. With the edge of a clean ruler or the blunt edge of a long knife, make several deep creases spaced 1-inch apart from one side of the loaf to the other. Cover and let rise in a warm oven 30 to 45 minutes until doubled in size. (*Hint:* To

warm oven slightly, turn oven on. Warm setting for 1 minute, then turn it off, and place covered dough in oven to rise. Remove pan from oven before preheating.)

5. Bake for 20 to 25 minutes until golden. Remove from oven and serve warm with butter.

Yields 1 loaf

BAKE CYCLE: Dough

NUTRITIONAL INFORMATION PER SLICE
Calories 112 / Fat 1.3 grams / Carbohydrates 21.7 grams / Protein 2.9 grams / Fiber .9 grams / Sodium 305 milligrams / Cholesterol 0 milligrams

---

Michael's Onion Rye Bread

When Lois's son Michael comes to visit, she bakes this bread for him. It has a very welcoming aroma. Serve this tasty rye slightly warm to enjoy it at its best.

	SMALL	MEDIUM	LARGE
WATER	¾ to ⅞ cup	1⅛ to 1¼ cups	1¾ to 1⅞ cups
OIL	2 teaspoons	1 tablespoon	4 teaspoons
MOLASSES	2 teaspoons	1 tablespoon	4 teaspoons
SALT	1 teaspoon	1½ teaspoons	2 teaspoons
WHOLE WHEAT FLOUR	1 cup	1½ cups	2 cups
BREAD FLOUR	1 cup	1½ cups	2 cups
RYE FLOUR	½ cup	¾ cup	1 cup
VITAL WHEAT GLUTEN, OPTIONAL	2 tablespoons	3 tablespoons to ⅓ cup	4 tablespoons
MINCED FRESH ONION	¼ cup	⅓ cup	½ cup
CARAWAY SEEDS	1 teaspoon	1 teaspoon	2 teaspoons
RED STAR BRAND ACTIVE DRY YEAST	1½ teaspoons	2 teaspoons	2½ teaspoons

1. Place all ingredients in bread pan, using the least amount of liquid listed in the recipe. Select Medium Crust setting and Whole Wheat cycle. Press Start.

2. Observe the dough as it kneads. After 5 to 10 minutes, if it appears dry and stiff or if your machine sounds as if it's straining to knead it, add more liquid 1 tablespoon at a time until dough forms a smooth, soft, pliable ball that is slightly tacky to the touch.

3. After the baking cycle ends, remove bread from pan, place on cake rack, and allow to cool 1 hour before slicing.

CRUST: Medium
BAKE CYCLE: Whole Wheat
OPTIONAL BAKE CYCLES: Standard / Delayed Timer / Rapid Bake

NUTRITIONAL INFORMATION PER SLICE
Calories 127 / Fat 1.5 grams / Carbohydrates 25 grams / Protein 3.9 grams / Fiber 3 grams / Sodium 230 milligrams / Cholesterol 0 milligrams

Microwave Lemon Curd

You can also purchase lemon curd in either the jam/jelly section of your market or the gourmet/imported foods area.

½ cup unsalted butter	Finely grated zest of 3 lemons
1 cup sugar	½ cup fresh lemon juice
3 eggs	

1. In a microwave-proof bowl, melt butter on HIGH in the microwave for 1 to 2 minutes.

2. In another bowl, combine sugar, eggs, lemon zest, and fresh lemon juice; blend with a wire whisk.

3. Slowly whisk in the hot melted butter.

4. Microwave on HIGH 3 to 4 minutes until thickened to a thin pudding consistency, whisking well after each minute.

5. Pour into a clean glass jar and store up to 2 weeks in the refrigerator or pour into sterilized jars and seal.

Yields about 2 cups

Midnight Sun Bread

T*his is an outstanding bread! It has a delicate, cakelike texture and combines the orange and caraway flavors that are popular in so many Scandinavian breads. It's also good toasted.*

	SMALL	MEDIUM	LARGE
BUTTERMILK	¾ to ⅞ cup	1⅛ to 1¼ cups	1½ to 1⅝ cups
HONEY	1½ tablespoons	2 tablespoons	3 tablespoons
SALT	1 teaspoon	1½ teaspoons	2 teaspoons
BUTTER OR MARGARINE	1½ tablespoons	2 tablespoons	3 tablespoons
BREAD FLOUR	2 cups	3 cups	4 cups
GRATED ORANGE RIND	of ½ orange	of 1 small orange	of 1 large orange
CARAWAY SEEDS	1 teaspoon	1½ teaspoons	2 teaspoons
RAISINS	⅓ cup	½ cup	⅔ cup
RED STAR BRAND ACTIVE DRY YEAST	1½ teaspoons	2 teaspoons	2½ teaspoons

I. Place all ingredients in bread pan, using the least amount of liquid listed in the recipe. Select Light Crust setting and press Start.

2. Observe the dough as it kneads. After 5 to 10 minutes, if it appears dry and stiff or if your machine sounds as if it's straining to knead it, add more liquid 1 tablespoon at a time until dough forms a smooth, soft, pliable ball that is slightly tacky to the touch.

3. After the baking cycle ends, remove bread from pan, place on cake rack, and allow to cool 1 hour before slicing.

CRUST: Light
BAKE CYCLE: Standard
OPTIONAL BAKE CYCLES: Sweet Bread / Raisin/Nut

NUTRITIONAL INFORMATION PER SLICE
Calories 149 / Fat 2.1 grams / Carbohydrates 28.9 grams / Protein 3.8 grams / Fiber 1.3 grams / Sodium 270 milligrams / Cholesterol .7 milligrams

---

Oatmeal Bread

This bakes up into a gorgeous, tall loaf in most machines and has an unmistakable, wholesome oatmeal flavor. It's a wonderful sandwich bread.

	SMALL	MEDIUM	LARGE
OLD-FASHIONED OATS	⅔ cup	1 cup	1⅓ cups
BUTTERMILK	⅞ to 1 cup	1⅜ to 1½ cups + 1 tablespoon	1¾ to 1⅞ cups
HONEY	2 tablespoons	3 tablespoons	¼ cup
SALT	1 teaspoon	1½ teaspoons	2 teaspoons
BUTTER OR MARGARINE	1½ tablespoons	2 tablespoons	3 tablespoons
BREAD FLOUR	2 cups	3 cups	4 cups
RED STAR BRAND ACTIVE DRY YEAST	1½ teaspoons	2 teaspoons	2½ teaspoons

I. Place all ingredients in bread pan, using the least amount of liquid listed in the recipe. Select Medium Crust setting and press Start.

2. Observe the dough as it kneads. After 5 to 10 minutes, if it appears dry and stiff or if your machine sounds as if it's straining to knead it, add more liquid 1 tablespoon at a time until dough forms a smooth, soft, pliable ball that is slightly tacky to the touch.

3. After the baking cycle ends, remove bread from pan, place on cake rack, and allow to cool 1 hour before slicing.

CRUST: Medium
BAKE CYCLE: Standard
OPTIONAL BAKE CYCLES: Whole Wheat / Sweet Bread / Rapid Bake

NUTRITIONAL INFORMATION PER SLICE
Calories 159 / Fat 2.5 grams / Carbohydrates 29.2 grams / Protein 4.7 grams / Fiber 1.5 grams / Sodium 269 milligrams / Cholesterol 5.3 milligrams

Orange Bubble Loaf

Serve this at a holiday brunch or on Christmas morning for a sure-fire crowd pleaser. To eat, pull away the sugary, orange-crusted rounds of dough from this attractive coffee cake.

DOUGH

	SMALL	MEDIUM	LARGE
MILK	¼ cup	⅜ cup	⅜ cup
WATER	¼ cup	⅜ cup	⅜ cup
EGG	1	1	2
SALT	1 teaspoon	1 teaspoon	1½ teaspoons
BUTTER OR MARGARINE	3 tablespoons	4 tablespoons	6 tablespoons
SUGAR	¼ cup	⅓ cup	½ cup
GRATED LEMON RIND	of ½ lemon	of ½ lemon	of 1 lemon
ALL-PURPOSE FLOUR	2 cups	3 cups	4 cups
RED STAR BRAND ACTIVE DRY YEAST	1½ teaspoons	1½ teaspoons	2 teaspoons

GLAZE

	SMALL	MEDIUM	LARGE
MELTED BUTTER OR MARGARINE	¼ cup	¼ cup	½ cup
SUGAR	½ cup	½ cup	1 cup
GRATED ORANGE RIND	of 2 oranges	of 2 oranges	of 4 oranges

1. Place dough ingredients in bread pan, select Dough setting, and press Start.

2. When the dough has risen long enough, the machine will beep. Turn off bread machine, remove bread pan, and turn out dough onto a lightly floured countertop or cutting board.

For the Small Recipe
Brush one 8½x4½x2½-inch loaf pan with some of the melted butter needed for the glaze.

For the Medium Recipe

Brush a 10-inch ring mold with some of the melted butter needed for the glaze.

For the Large Recipe

Brush two 8½x4½x2½-inch loaf pans with some of the melted butter needed for the glaze. With a sharp knife, divide dough in half.

3. In a small bowl, combine remaining melted butter, sugar, and grated orange rind for the glaze. Pinch off small pieces of dough about the size of an acorn, and roll into balls. Roll each in the glaze and then place in prepared pan. Cover and let rise in a warm oven 30 to 45 minutes until doubled in size. (*Hint:* To warm oven slightly, turn oven on Warm setting for 1 minute, then turn it off, and place covered dough in oven to rise. Remove pan from oven before preheating.)

4. Preheat oven to 350°F. Bake for 30 minutes until golden. Remove from oven, turn out onto a plate, and then invert onto serving plate. Serve warm.

Small recipe yields one 8x4-inch coffee cake
Medium recipe yields one 10-inch round coffee cake
Large recipe yields two 8x4-inch coffee cakes

BAKE CYCLE: Dough

NUTRITIONAL INFORMATION PER SLICE
Calories 212 / Fat 7.2 grams / Carbohydrates 33.3 grams / Protein 3.6 grams / Fiber .9 grams / Sodium 237 milligrams / Cholesterol 15.5 milligrams

---

Pizza Dough

Now *you can have delicious homemade pizza in the wink of an eye! And should you change your mind at the last minute, you can keep the dough in an oiled plastic bag for several days in the refrigerator.*

	SMALL	MEDIUM	LARGE
WATER	⅝ to ¾ cup	⅞ to 1 cup	1⅛ to 1¼ cups
OLIVE OIL	1½ tablespoons	2 tablespoons	3 tablespoons
SALT	½ teaspoon	1 teaspoon	1 teaspoon
SUGAR	2 teaspoons	1 tablespoon	4 teaspoons
ALL-PURPOSE FLOUR	2 cups	3 cups	4 cups
RED STAR BRAND ACTIVE DRY YEAST	2 teaspoons	2 teaspoons	2½ teaspoons

1. Place dough ingredients in bread pan, select Dough setting, and press Start.

2. When the dough has risen long enough, the machine will beep. Turn off bread machine, remove bread pan, and turn out dough onto a lightly floured countertop or cutting board. Form dough into a mound and allow it to rest for 10 minutes.

For the Small Recipe

Grease one 14-inch pizza pan. With your hands, gently stretch and press dough to fit evenly into pan. Pinch dough around the edges to form small rim.

For the Medium Recipe

Grease one deep-dish or two 12-inch pizza pans. If using two pans, cut dough in half with a sharp knife. With your hands, gently stretch and press dough to fit evenly into pan(s). Pinch dough around the edges to form small rim.

For the Large Recipe

Grease two 12- or 14-inch pizza pans. With sharp knife, divide dough in half.

With your hands, gently stretch and press dough to fit evenly into pans. Pinch dough around the edges to form small rim.

3. Spread your favorite pizza sauce on top of the dough, then add toppings of your choice, except cheese. Preheat oven to 450 F.

4. Bake for 15 to 20 minutes. Sprinkle with cheese the last five minutes of baking. When cheese melts, remove from oven, slice into wedges, and serve hot. (*Note:* For a lighter, chewier crust, reduce the oven temperature to 400°F.)

Small recipe yields one thin-crust 14-inch pizza
Medium recipe yields one deep-dish pizza or two 12-inch pizzas
Large recipe yields two 12- or 14-inch pizzas

BAKE CYCLE: Dough

NUTRITIONAL INFORMATION PER SLICE
Calories 119 / Fat 2.2 grams / Carbohydrates 21.3 grams / Protein 2.9 grams / Fiber .8 grams / Sodium 153 milligrams / Cholesterol 0 milligrams

Quaker Multigrain Bread

*Q*uaker *now makes a multigrain cereal that looks much like their famous oats but it's a combination of rye, barley, oats, and wheat flakes. We think this new cereal is a perfect ingredient to add to your breads. (Note: This is a small loaf. If you choose to add gluten, increase the buttermilk by 1 or 2 tablespoons as well.)*

	SMALL	MEDIUM	LARGE
QUAKER MULTIGRAIN CEREAL	⅔ cup	1 cup	1⅓ cups
BUTTERMILK	⅜ to ⅞ cup	1¼ to 1⅜ cups + 1 tablespoon	1⅝ to 1¾ cups
MOLASSES	2 tablespoons	3 tablespoons	¼ cup
SALT	1 teaspoon	1½ teaspoons	2 teaspoons
BUTTER OR MARGARINE	1 tablespoon	1½ tablespoons	2 tablespoons
BREAD FLOUR	1⅓ cups	2 cups	2⅔ cups
WHOLE WHEAT FLOUR	⅓ cup	½ cup	⅔ cup
VITAL WHEAT GLUTEN, OPTIONAL	2 tablespoons	3 tablespoons	¼ cup
RED STAR BRAND ACTIVE DRY YEAST	1½ teaspoons	2 teaspoons	2½ teaspoons

1. Place all ingredients in bread pan, using the least amount of liquid listed in the recipe. Select Medium Crust setting and press Start.

2. Observe the dough as it kneads. After 5 to 10 minutes, if it appears dry and stiff or if your machine sounds as if it's straining to knead it, add more liquid 1 tablespoon at a time until dough forms a smooth, soft, pliable ball that is slightly tacky to the touch.

3. After the baking cycle ends, remove bread from pan, place on cake rack, and allow to cool 1 hour before slicing.

CRUST: Medium

BAKE CYCLE: Standard

OPTIONAL BAKE CYCLES: Whole Wheat / Sweet Bread / Rapid Bake

NUTRITIONAL INFORMATION PER SLICE

Calories 139 / Fat 1.9 grams / Carbohydrates 26 grams / Protein 5.2 grams / Fiber 1.4 grams / Sodium 264 milligrams / Cholesterol 4.1 milligrams

Sally Lunn Bread

Here's an egg bread so sweet it almost tastes like a pound cake. We can picture it on a silver tray with a bowl of strawberries and a pitcher of cream.

	SMALL	MEDIUM	LARGE
HEAVY CREAM	⅛ cup	¼ cup	¼ cup
WATER	⅛ to ¼ cup	¼ to ⅜ cup	¼ to ⅜ cup
EGGS	2	3	4
SALT	½ teaspoon	1 teaspoon	1 teaspoon
BUTTER OR MARGARINE, CUT IN PIECES	¼ cup	⅓ cup	½ cup
SUGAR	3 tablespoons	¼ cup	6 tablespoons
ALL-PURPOSE FLOUR	2 cups	3 cups	4 cups
RED STAR BRAND ACTIVE DRY YEAST	1½ teaspoons	2 teaspoons	2½ teaspoons

1. Place all ingredients in bread pan, using the least amount of liquid listed in the recipe. Select Light Crust setting and Sweet Bread cycle. Press Start.

2. Observe the dough as it kneads. After 5 to 10 minutes, if it appears dry and stiff or if your machine sounds as if it's straining to knead it, add more liquid 1 tablespoon at a time until dough forms a smooth, soft, pliable ball that is slightly tacky to the touch.

3. After the baking cycle ends, remove bread from pan, place on cake rack, and allow to cool 1 hour before slicing.

CRUST: Light
BAKE CYCLE: Sweet Bread
OPTIONAL BAKE CYCLES: Whole Wheat / Standard

> NUTRITIONAL INFORMATION PER SLICE
> Calories 181 / Fat 7.2 grams / Carbohydrates 24.3 grams / Protein 4.3 grams / Fiber .8 grams / Sodium 218 milligrams / Cholesterol 51.1 milligrams

San Diego Sunshine

*J*ust *like our hometown, this bread will delight your senses! It's a sweet whole wheat loaf with a delicate hint of orange. Pack up a picnic basket with a Thermos of hot coffee or tea, a loaf of this bread, and some honey butter. Locate a city park or a sunny terrace and you'll have the makings for a romantic, leisurely breakfast.*

	SMALL	MEDIUM	LARGE
WATER	¾ to ⅞ cup	1 to 1⅛ cups	1⅜ to 1½ cups
HONEY	1 tablespoon	2 tablespoons	2 tablespoons
SALT	1 teaspoon	1 teaspoon	2 teaspoons
BUTTER OR MARGARINE	1½ tablespoons	2 tablespoons	3 tablespoons
BROWN SUGAR	1 tablespoon	2 tablespoons	2 tablespoons
BREAD FLOUR	1⅓ cups	2 cups	2⅔ cups
WHOLE WHEAT FLOUR	⅔ cup	1 cup	1⅓ cups
GRATED ORANGE RIND	of 1 orange	of 1½ oranges	of 2 oranges
RED STAR BRAND ACTIVE DRY YEAST	1½ teaspoons	2 teaspoons	2½ teaspoons

1. Place all ingredients in bread pan, using the least amount of liquid listed in the recipe. Select Light Crust setting and press Start.

2. Observe the dough as it kneads. After 5 to 10 minutes, if it appears dry and stiff or if your machine sounds as if it's straining to knead it, add more liquid 1 tablespoon at a time until dough forms a smooth, soft, pliable ball that is slightly tacky to the touch.

3. After the baking cycle ends, remove bread from pan, place on cake rack, and allow to cool 1 hour before slicing.

CRUST: Light

BAKE CYCLE: Standard

OPTIONAL BAKE CYCLES: Sweet Bread / Delayed Timer

NUTRITIONAL INFORMATION PER SLICE
Calories 127 / Fat 1.9 grams / Carbohydrates 24.6 grams / Protein 3.2 grams / Fiber 1.7 grams / Sodium 169 milligrams / Cholesterol 4.4 milligrams

San Francisco Sourdough French Bread

*M*ost people love the tangy, tart taste of sourdough. If you can't get to San Francisco for the real thing, this will do in a pinch. (Note: Starters vary in their consistency. If yours is thin, use the lesser amount of water listed in the recipe.)

	SMALL	MEDIUM	LARGE
WATER	¼ to ⅜ cup	½ to ⅝ cup	¾ to ⅞ cup
SOURDOUGH STARTER	¾ cup	1 cup	1½ cups
SALT	1 teaspoon	1 teaspoon	2 teaspoons
SUGAR	1 teaspoon	1 teaspoon	2 teaspoons
BREAD FLOUR	2 cups	3 cups	4 cups
RED STAR BRAND ACTIVE DRY YEAST	2 teaspoons	2 teaspoons	2½ teaspoons

For a Mild Sourdough

1. Place all ingredients in bread pan, select Dough setting, and press Start.

For the Sourest Sourdough

1. In a medium bowl, combine the water, starter, and half the flour. Cover and let stand in a warm place up to 24 hours until very sour and bubbly. Then combine the mixture with the remaining ingredients in the bread pan, select Dough setting, and press Start.

2. When the dough has risen long enough, the machine will beep. Turn off bread machine, remove bread pan, and turn out dough onto a lightly floured countertop or cutting board.

For the Small Recipe
Shape dough into one 10-inch oblong loaf or one round loaf or one 24-inch-long thin baguette or 6 French rolls.

For the Medium Recipe
Shape dough into one 12-inch oblong loaf or one large round loaf or two 18-inch-long thin baguettes or 8 French rolls.

For the Large Recipe

Shape dough into two 10-inch oblong loaves or two round loaves or two 24-inch-long thin baguettes or 12 French rolls.

3. Place loaf (loaves) on a baking sheet that is well greased or sprinkled with cornmeal. With a sharp knife or razor blade, slash the rolls or the baguettes straight down the center about ½ inch deep. On the oblong loaf, make three diagonal ashes. On the round loaf, slash an x or # on top. Let rise in a warm oven 30 to 45 minutes until doubled in size (*Hint:* To warm oven slightly, turn on Warm setting for 1 minute, then turn it off, and place covered dough in oven to rise. Remove pan from oven before preheating.)

4. Preheat oven to 400°F. With a plant mister, mist each loaf with water (or brush with water). Bake for 25 to 30 minutes until golden brown, misting with water twice more at 5-minute intervals. Remove from oven and cool on wire racks. To preserve the crisp crust, do not store in plastic wrap or bags. Bread can be loosely covered or left out for up to 2 days before it dries out completely.

Small recipe yields 1 loaf or 6 rolls
Medium recipe yields 1 loaf, 2 baguettes, or 8 rolls
Large recipe yields 2 loaves or 12 rolls

BAKE CYCLE: Dough

NUTRITIONAL INFORMATION PER SLICE
Calories 119 / Fat .3 grams / Carbohydrates 25.3 grams / Protein 3.7 grams / Fiber 1 gram / Sodium 155 milligrams / Cholesterol .1 milligrams

Shareen's Whole Wheat Pizza Crust

When the other cheerleaders are tossing little Shareen in the air, I wonder if she's thinking about this whole wheat pizza crust. Probably not, even though it's her favorite. More likely she's just contemplating her landing. However, we think of it often when the idea of having pizza for dinner comes to mind. We found this whole wheat crust added a new dimension to our homemade pizzas . . . a delightful "earthy" flavor.

	SMALL	MEDIUM	LARGE
WATER	¾ cup	1 cup	1⅜ cups
SALT	1 teaspoon	1 teaspoon	1½ teaspoons
OLIVE OIL	1½ tablespoons	2 tablespoons	3 tablespoons
SUGAR	1 teaspoon	1½ teaspoons	2 teaspoons
WHOLE WHEAT FLOUR	2 cups	3 cups	4 cups
RED STAR BRAND ACTIVE DRY YEAST	1½ teaspoons	1½ teaspoons	2 teaspoons

1. Place dough ingredients in bread pan, select Dough setting, and press Start.

2. When the dough has risen long enough, the machine will beep. Turn off bread machine, remove bread pan, and turn out dough onto a lightly floured countertop or cutting board. Form dough into a mound and allow it to rest for 10 minutes.

For the Small Recipe
Grease one 14-inch pizza pan. With your hands, gently stretch and press dough to fit evenly into pan.

For the Medium Recipe
Grease one deep dish or two 12- to 14-inch pizza pans. If using two pans, cut dough in half with a sharp knife. With your hands, gently stretch and press dough to fit evenly into the pan(s).

For the Large Recipe
Grease two 14- or 16-inch pizza pans. With your hands, gently stretch and press dough to fit evenly into the pans.

3. Spread your favorite pizza sauce on top of the dough, then add toppings of your choice, except cheese.

4. Preheat oven to 450°F. Bake for 15 to 20 minutes. Sprinkle cheese on top of hot pizza as soon as you remove it from the oven. Serve hot.

Small recipe yields one 14-inch pizza
Medium recipe yields one deep-dish pizza or two 12- or 14-inch pizzas
Large recipe yields two 14- or 16-inch pizzas

BAKE CYCLE: Dough

NUTRITIONAL INFORMATION PER ⅛ SLICE, SMALL-SIZE CRUST
Calories 112 / Fat 1.4 grams / Carbohydrates 22.3 grams / Protein 4.3 grams / Fiber 3.9 grams / Sodium 268 milligrams / Cholesterol 0 milligrams

NUTRITIONAL INFORMATION PER ⅛ SLICE, MEDIUM-SIZE CRUST
Calories 127 / Fat 3.1 grams / Carbohydrates 22.3 grams / Protein 4.3 grams / Fiber 3.9 grams / Sodium 269 milligrams / Cholesterol 0 milligrams

NUTRITIONAL INFORMATION PER ⅛ SLICE, LARGE-SIZE CRUST
Calories 254 / Fat 6.2 grams / Carbohydrates 44.6 grams / Protein 8.4 grams / Fiber 7.8 grams / Sodium 403 milligrams / Cholesterol 0 milligrams

---

Shayna's Vegan Burgers

*T*hese hearty "burgers" came in mighty handy when Linda's daughter Shayna needed something quick to pack for lunch. There are endless combinations of filling ingredients you can try. If you have a little filling left over, it can be chilled and served as a main dish salad; frozen and served as a side dish some other day; or rolled up in a tortilla for a lunch burrito or tasty wrap.

DOUGH

	SMALL	MEDIUM	LARGE
WATER	¾ cup	1 cup	1⅜ cups
SALT	¾ teaspoon	1 teaspoon	1½ teaspoons
OLIVE OIL	1½ tablespoons	2 tablespoons	3 tablespoons
SUGAR	2 tablespoons	3 tablespoons	¼ cup
ALL-PURPOSE FLOUR	1 cup	1½ cups	2 cups
WHOLE WHEAT FLOUR	1 cup	1½ cups	2 cups
RED STAR BRAND ACTIVE DRY YEAST	2 teaspoons	2 teaspoons	2½ teaspoons

FILLING

	SMALL	MEDIUM	LARGE
FRESHLY COOKED OR CANNED BLACK BEANS, RINSED, DRAINED	1⅓ cups	2 cups	2⅔ cups
FROZEN CORN KERNELS, THAWED, DRAINED	1⅓ cups	2 cups	2⅔ cups
COOKED BROWN RICE	1⅓ cups	2 cups	2⅔ cups
CHOPPED GREEN PEPPER	⅓ cup (about ½ small pepper)	½ cup (about ½ large pepper)	⅔ cup (about 1 small pepper)
GROUND CUMIN	1½ teaspoons	2 teaspoons	1 tablespoon
CHILI POWDER	¾ teaspoon	1 teaspoon	1½ teaspoon
SALT (OPTIONAL)	¾ teaspoon	1 teaspoon	1½ teaspoons
SALSA	⅓ cup	½ cup	⅔ cup

I. Place dough ingredients in bread pan, select Dough setting, and press Start.

2. Meanwhile, in a large bowl, combine filling ingredients. Set aside. Grease a large baking sheet.

3. When the dough has risen long enough, the machine will beep. Turn off bread

machine, remove bread pan, and turn out dough onto a lightly floured countertop or cutting board. Gently roll or stretch dough into a 12-inch rope.

For the Small Recipe

With a sharp knife, divide dough into 8 pieces.

For the Medium Recipe

With a sharp knife, divide dough into 12 pieces.

For the Large Recipe

With a sharp knife, divide dough into 16 pieces.

4. With a rolling pin, roll each piece into a 6-inch circle. Place ½ cup filling mixture in the center of each circle. Pull the edges up to meet in the center and pinch dough together well to seal. Place on prepared baking sheet, sealed-side down. Cover and let rise in a warm oven 15 minutes. (*Hint:* To warm slightly, turn oven on Warm setting for 1 minute, then turn it off, and place covered dough in oven to rise. Remove baking sheet from oven to preheat.)

5. Preheat oven to 400°F. Bake for 15 to 20 minutes until brown. Remove from oven and serve warm or place on cake rack to cool. Serve warm or cold with additional salsa and/or guacamole. These freeze well in a plastic bag for up to 3 months. To reheat, place in a 325°F oven for 30 minutes or microwave on HIGH power for 1½ to 2 minutes.

FILLING VARIATIONS:

Vegetables: Cooked carrots, broccoli, celery, cabbage, onions, peas, spinach, turnips, potatoes, etc.

Grains: Cooked couscous, tabouleh, wild rice, white rice, bulgur, kasha, etc.

Legumes: Cooked or canned kidney beans, garbanzo beans, pinto beans, lima beans, lentils, split peas, etc.

Seasonings: Curry powder, lemon pepper, chili powder, freshly ground pepper, various herbs, barbeque sauce, spaghetti sauce, hummus, tahini, etc.

Small recipe yields 8 burgers
Medium recipe yields 12 burgers
Large recipe yields 16 burgers

BAKE CYCLE: Dough

NUTRITIONAL INFORMATION PER BURGER
Calories 115 / Fat .3 grams / Carbohydrates 23.9 grams / Protein 3.4 grams / Fiber .9 grams / Sodium 230 milligrams / Cholesterol 0 milligrams

---

Sour Rye Bread

We think this combination of sour cream and rye is a winner. This slightly tangy loaf baked up quite differently from machine to machine. In some it was a real dome thumper, in others it needed added gluten. Try it the first time without adding extra gluten. If need be, add gluten to future loaves if the trial loaf bakes up small.

	SMALL	MEDIUM	LARGE
WATER	⅝ to ¾ cup	⅞ to 1 cup	1⅛ to 1¼ cups
SOUR CREAM	¼ cup	½ cup	½ cup
SALT	1 teaspoon	1½ teaspoons	2 teaspoons
SUGAR	1½ tablespoons	2 tablespoons	3 tablespoons
BREAD FLOUR	1⅓ cups	2¼ cups	2⅔ cups
RYE FLOUR	⅔ cup	1 cup	1⅓ cups
CARAWAY SEEDS	2 teaspoons	1 tablespoon	4 teaspoons
VITAL WHEAT GLUTEN (OPTIONAL)	2 tablespoons	3 tablespoons	¼ cup
RED STAR BRAND ACTIVE DRY YEAST	1½ teaspoons	2 teaspoons	2½ teaspoons

1. Place all ingredients in bread pan, using the least amount of liquid listed in the recipe. Select Medium crust setting and Whole Wheat cycle. Press Start.

2. Observe the dough as it kneads. After 5 to 10 minutes, if it appears dry and stiff or if your machine sounds as if it's straining to knead it, add more liquid 1 tablespoon at a time until dough forms a smooth, soft, pliable ball that is slightly tacky to the touch

3. After the baking cycle ends, remove bread from pan, place on cake rack, and allow to cool 1 hour before slicing.

CRUST: Medium
BAKE CYCLE: Whole Wheat
OPTIONAL BAKE CYCLES: Standard / Sweet Bread

NUTRITIONAL INFORMATION PER SLICE
Calories 134 / Fat 2.2 grams / Carbohydrates 24.2 grams / Protein 4 grams / Fiber 1.8 grams / Sodium 234 milligrams / Cholesterol 3.6 milligrams

---

Squaw Bread

When dining out, we've always enjoyed this sweet whole wheat and rye bread. Don't overlook the first step. Purée the liquids and sweeteners in the blender before adding them to the bread pan.

	SMALL	MEDIUM	LARGE
MILK	⅜ cup	⅝ cup	⅞ cup
WATER	⅜ to ½ cup	⅝ to ¾ cup	⅞ to 1 cup
OIL	1½ tablespoons	2 tablespoons	3 tablespoons
HONEY	1 tablespoon	1½ tablespoons	2 tablespoons
RAISINS	1½ tablespoons	2 tablespoons	3 tablespoons
BROWN SUGAR	1½ tablespoons	2 tablespoons	3 tablespoons
BREAD FLOUR	1 cup	1½ cups	2 cups
WHOLE WHEAT FLOUR	¾ cup	1¼ cups	1½ cups
RYE FLOUR	½ cup	¾ cup	1 cup
VITAL WHEAT GLUTEN (OPTIONAL)	2 tablespoons	3 tablespoons to ⅓ cup	4 tablespoons
RED STAR BRAND ACTIVE DRY YEAST	1½ teaspoons	2 teaspoons	2½ teaspoons

1. In a blender, liquefy the milk, water, oil, honey, raisins, and brown sugar on high speed. Combine mixture with rest of ingredients in bread pan, select Medium Crust setting and Whole Wheat cycle. Press Start.

2. Observe the dough as it kneads. After 5 to 10 minutes, if it appears dry and stiff or if your machine sounds as if it's straining to knead it, add more liquid 1 tablespoon at a time until dough forms a smooth, soft, pliable ball that is slightly tacky to the touch.

3. After the baking cycle ends, remove bread from pan, place on cake rack, and allow to cool 1 hour before slicing.

CRUST: Medium

BAKE CYCLE: Whole Wheat

OPTIONAL BAKE CYCLES: Standard / Sweet Bread

NUTRITIONAL INFORMATION PER SLICE
Calories 146 / Fat 2.5 grams / Carbohydrates 27.7 grams / Protein 3.9 grams / Fiber 2.7 grams / Sodium 160 milligrams / Cholesterol .4 milligrams

Sweet Lelani Bread

his Hawaiian-style bread is a spectacular addition to any luncheon buffet. It's moist, light, and elegant. Don't let the long list of ingredients prevent you from trying this bread. It's definitely one of the best in the book. Keep an eye on it first time you make it; it's a high riser in some machines.

	SMALL	MEDIUM	LARGE
CANNED PINEAPPLE CHUNKS, CUT UP AND WELL DRAINED (RESERVE JUICE)	⅓ cup	½ cup	⅔ cup
BUTTERMILK	3 to 4 tablespoons	¼ to ⅜ cup	⅜ to ½ cup
RESERVED PINEAPPLE JUICE	2 tablespoons	¼ cup	¼ cup
EGG	1	1	2
SLICED VERY RIPE BANANA	⅓ cup	½ cup	⅔ cup
SALT	1 teaspoon	1 teaspoon	2 teaspoons
BUTTER OR MARGARINE	2 tablespoons	3 tablespoons	¼ cup
SUGAR	1 tablespoon	1½ tablespoons	2 tablespoons
BREAD FLOUR	2 cups	3 cups	4 cups
WHOLE WHEAT FLOUR	3 tablespoons	¼ cup	6 tablespoons
SHREDDED COCONUT	⅓ cup	½ cup	⅔ cup
CHOPPED MACADAMIA NUTS	¼ cup	⅓ cup	½ cup
RED STAR BRAND ACTIVE DRY YEAST	1½ teaspoons	2 teaspoons	2½ teaspoons

I. Place all ingredients in bread pan, using the least amount of liquid listed in the recipe. Select Light Crust setting and press Start.

2. Observe the dough as it kneads. After 5 to 10 minutes, if it appears dry and stiff or if your machine sounds as if it's straining to knead it, add more liquid 1 tablespoon at a time until dough forms a smooth, soft, pliable ball that is slightly tacky to the touch.

3. After the baking cycle ends, remove bread from pan, place on cake rack, and allow to cool 1 hour before slicing.

CRUST: Light

BAKE CYCLE: Standard

OPTIONAL BAKE CYCLES: Whole Wheat / Sweet Bread / Raisin/Nut

NUTRITIONAL INFORMATION PER SLICE
Calories 191 / Fat 6.8 grams / Carbohydrates 28.7 grams / Protein 4.2 grams / Fiber 1.8 grams / Sodium 215 milligrams / Cholesterol 22 milligrams

---

Sweet Milk Bread

*T*his is a wonderful, soft, finely textured white bread with a rich, sweet taste. Even served up plain, it's very munchable bread.

	SMALL	MEDIUM	LARGE
WATER	⅝ cup	⅞ to 1 cup	1⅛ to 1¼ cups
SWEETENED CONDENSED MILK	⅜ cup	½ cup	⅝ cup
SALT	1 teaspoon	1 teaspoon	1½ teaspoons
BUTTER OR MARGARINE	1 tablespoon	1 tablespoon	2 tablespoons
BREAD FLOUR	2 cups	3⅓ cups	4 cups
RED STAR BRAND ACTIVE DRY YEAST	1½ teaspoons	2 teaspoons	2½ teaspoons

I. Place all ingredients in bread pan, using the least amount of liquid listed in the recipe. Select Light Crust setting and press Start.

2. Observe the dough as it kneads. After 5 to 10 minutes, if it appears dry and stiff or if your machine sounds as if it's straining to knead it, add more liquid 1 tablespoon at a time until dough forms a smooth, soft, pliable ball that is slightly tacky to the touch.

3. After the baking cycle ends, remove bread from pan, place on cake rack, and allow to cool 1 hour before slicing.

CRUST: Light
BAKE CYCLE: Standard
OPTIONAL BAKE CYCLES: Whole Wheat / Sweet Bread / Rapid Bake

NUTRITIONAL INFORMATION PER SLICE
Calories 151 / Fat 2.1 grams / Carbohydrates 28.4 grams / Protein 4 grams / Fiber .9 grams / Sodium 174 milligrams / Cholesterol 5.9 milligrams

Tomato Bread

T*here's no mistaking this one! It's a bright pumpkin color with a very definite tomato flavor. The aroma as it bakes is extraordinary! Leftovers make wonderful croutons.*

	SMALL	MEDIUM	LARGE
MILK	¼ to ⅜ cup	⅝ to ¾ cup	¾ to ⅞ cup
TOMATO PASTE	6 tablespoons	1 (6-ounce) can	¾ cup
EGG	1	1	2
OLIVE OIL	2 teaspoons	1 tablespoon	4 teaspoons
SALT	½ teaspoon	½ teaspoon	1 teaspoon
SUGAR	2 teaspoons	1 tablespoon	2 tablespoons
BREAD FLOUR	2 cups	3¼ cups	4 cups
ITALIAN SEASONING	½ teaspoon	1 teaspoon	1½ teaspoons
DRIED MINCED ONION	1½ teaspoons	2 teaspoons	1 tablespoon
GARLIC POWDER	¼ teaspoon	¼ teaspoon	½ teaspoon
GRATED NUTMEG	¼ teaspoon	½ teaspoon	½ teaspoon
RED STAR BRAND ACTIVE DRY YEAST	1½ teaspoons	2 teaspoons	2½ teaspoons

1. Place all ingredients in bread pan, using the least amount of liquid listed in the recipe. Select Light Crust setting and press Start.

2. Observe the dough as it kneads. After 5 to 10 minutes, if it appears dry and stiff or if your machine sounds as if it's straining to knead it, add more liquid 1 tablespoon at a time until dough forms a smooth, soft, pliable ball that is slightly tacky to the touch.

3. After the baking cycle ends, remove bread from pan, place on cake rack, and allow to cool 1 hour before slicing.

CRUST: Light

BAKE CYCLE: Standard

OPTIONAL BAKE CYCLES: Rapid Bake

NUTRITIONAL INFORMATION PER SLICE

Calories 140 / Fat 1.9 grams / Carbohydrates 26.2 grams / Protein 4.4 grams / Fiber 1.4 grams / Sodium 183 milligrams / Cholesterol 15.7 milligrams

---

Whole Wheat Cinnamon Raisin Bread

*T*his dark, rich bread is scrumptious! Try it for breakfast, either plain or toasted. (Note: If you have a machine with a regular baking cycle of under 3 hours, you may need to reduce the amount of butter by half or switch to the Whole Wheat cycle if you find it didn't rise well the first time.)

	SMALL	MEDIUM	LARGE
BUTTERMILK	⅝ to ¾ cup	⅞ to 1 cup + 1 tablespoon	1¼ to 1⅜ cups
EGG	1	1	2
SALT	¾ teaspoon	1 teaspoon	1½ teaspoons
BUTTER OR MARGARINE	¼ cup	⅓ cup	½ cup
BROWN SUGAR	2 tablespoons	3 tablespoons	¼ cup
WHOLE WHEAT FLOUR	1 cup	1½ cups	2 cups
BREAD FLOUR	1¼ cups	1½ cups	2½ cups
VITAL WHEAT GLUTEN (OPTIONAL)	2 tablespoons	3 tablespoons	¼ cup
RAISINS	½ cup	⅔ cup	1 cup
CINNAMON	¾ teaspoon	1 teaspoon	1½ teaspoons
RED STAR BRAND ACTIVE DRY YEAST	1½ teaspoons	2 teaspoons	2½ teaspoons

1. Place all ingredients in bread pan, using the least amount of liquid listed in the recipe. Select Medium Crust setting and press Start.

2. Observe the dough as it kneads. After 5 to 10 minutes, if it appears dry and stiff or if your machine sounds as if it's straining to knead it, add more liquid 1 tablespoon at a time until dough forms a smooth, soft, pliable ball that is slightly tacky to the touch.

3. After the baking cycle ends, remove bread from pan, place on cake rack, and allow to cool 1 hour before slicing.

CRUST: Medium

BAKE CYCLE: Standard

OPTIONAL BAKE CYCLES: Whole Wheat / Sweet Bread / Raisin/Nut

NUTRITIONAL INFORMATION PER SLICE
Calories 175 / Fat 5.2 grams / Carbohydrates 28.7 grams / Protein 4.5 grams / Fiber 2.5 grams / Sodium 212 milligrams / Cholesterol 27.5 milligrams

Whole Wheat Hamburger and Hot Dog Buns

These are definitely five-star hamburger buns. You'll never go back to the store-bought version once you've tried these.

	SMALL	MEDIUM	LARGE
WATER	⅝ cup	1 cup	1⅛ cup
EGG	1	1	2
SALT	½ teaspoon	¾ teaspoon	1 teaspoon
SHORTENING	3 tablespoons	¼ cup	6 tablespoons
SUGAR	3 tablespoons	¼ cup	6 tablespoons
ALL-PURPOSE FLOUR	1⅓ cups	2 cups	2⅔ cups
WHOLE WHEAT FLOUR	⅔ cup	1 cup	1⅓ cups
RED STAR BRAND ACTIVE DRY YEAST	2 teaspoons	3 teaspoons	4 teaspoons

1. Place dough ingredients in bread pan, select Dough setting, and press Start.

2. When the dough has risen long enough, the machine will beep. Turn off bread machine, remove bread pan, and turn out dough onto a lightly floured countertop or cutting board.

For the Small Recipe

With a sharp knife, divide dough into 7 pieces for hamburger buns or 8 pieces for hot dog buns.

For the Medium Recipe

With a sharp knife, divide dough into 10 pieces for hamburger buns or 12 pieces for hot dog buns.

For the Large Recipe

With a sharp knife, divide dough into 14 pieces for hamburger buns or 16 pieces for hot dog buns.

3. Grease a baking sheet. Roll pieces of dough into balls and flatten for hamburger buns or shape into 6-inch rolls for hot dog buns. Place on prepared baking sheet.

Cover and let rise in a warm oven 30 to 45 minutes until doubled in size. (*Hint:* To warm oven slightly, turn oven on Warm setting for 1 minute, then turn it off, and place covered dough in oven to rise. Remove pan from oven before preheating.)

4. Preheat oven to 400°F. Bake for 12 to 15 minutes until golden brown. Remove from oven and cool on racks. When ready to use, split buns in half horizontally. These will keep in a plastic bag in the freezer for 3 to 4 weeks.

Small recipe yields 7 hamburger or 8 hot dog buns
Medium recipe yields 10 hamburger or 12 hot dog buns
Large recipe yields 14 hamburger or 16 hot dog buns

BAKE CYCLE: Dough

NUTRITIONAL INFORMATION PER BUN
Calories 206 / Fat 6.1 grams / Carbohydrates 32.9 grams / Protein 5.1 grams / Fiber 2.4 grams / Sodium 168 milligrams / Cholesterol 21.3 milligrams

---

Whole Wheat Soda Bread

*C*hildren love this rich-tasting soda bread. It's one that rose quite high in our machines.

	SMALL	MEDIUM	LARGE
BUTTERMILK	⅞ to 1 cup	1¼ to 1⅜ cups	2⅛ to 2¼ cups
HONEY	1 tablespoon	1½ tablespoons	2 tablespoons
SALT	1 teaspoon	1½ teaspoons	2 teaspoons
BUTTER OR MARGARINE	1 tablespoon	1½ tablespoons	2 tablespoons
WHOLE WHEAT FLOUR	1⅓ cups	2 cups	2½ cups
BREAD FLOUR	⅔ cup	1 cup	1½ cups
VITAL WHEAT GLUTEN	2 tablespoons	3 tablespoons to ⅓ cup	¼ cup
BAKING SODA	¼ teaspoon	½ teaspoon	¾ teaspoon
RED STAR BRAND ACTIVE DRY YEAST	1½ teaspoons	2 teaspoons	2½ teaspoons

I. Place all ingredients in bread pan, using the least amount of liquid listed in the recipe. Select Medium Crust setting and Whole Wheat cycle. Press Start.

2. Observe the dough as it kneads. After 5 to 10 minutes, if it appears dry and stiff or if your machine sounds as if it's straining to knead it, add more liquid 1 tablespoon at a time until dough forms a smooth, soft, pliable ball that is slightly tacky to the touch.

3. After the baking cycle ends, remove bread from pan, place on cake rack, and allow to cool 1 hour before slicing.

CRUST: Medium
BAKE CYCLE: Whole Wheat
OPTIONAL BAKE CYCLES: Standard

NUTRITIONAL INFORMATION PER SLICE
Calories 125 / Fat 1.8 grams / Carbohydrates 23.1 grams / Protein 4.9 grams / Fiber 2.5 grams / Sodium 296 milligrams / Cholesterol .8 milligrams

SUGGESTED USES

We've had several requests to include this section again. These suggestions might help you select which bread to give as a gift, which one would be good to take to a potluck supper, etc.

SANDWICH BREADS

DeDe's Buttermilk Bread
Whole Wheat Hamburger
   and Hot Dog Buns
Lois's Country Crunch Bread
Quaker Multigrain Bread
French Bread Extraordinaire!
Anadama Bread
Heavenly Whole Wheat Bread
Lorraine's Buttermilk Rye Bread
Black Forest Pumpernickel
Honey 'n' Oats Bread

Buttermilk Honey Bran Bread
Sweet Milk Bread
Applesauce Rye Bread
Oatmeal Bread
Dennis's Multigrain Bread
Sour Rye Bread
San Francisco Sourdough Bread
Buttermilk Cracked-Wheat Bread
Michael's Onion Rye Bread
Whole Wheat Soda Bread
Egg Bread

BREAKFAST BREADS OR TOAST

San Diego Sunshine Bread
Jim's Cinnamon Rolls
Anne and Bill's Apple Oatmeal Bread
   with Raisins
Sweet Lelani Bread
Jim's Maple Walnut Bread
Linda's Lemon Bread
Jana's Seed and Nut Bread
Midnight Sun Bread
Marmalade and Oats Bread
Irene's Bavarian Coffee Cake

Whole Wheat Cinnamon Raisin
   Bread
Dawn's Vanilla Raisin Bread
Applesauce Rye Bread
Oatmeal Bread
Dennis's Multigrain Bread
Sour Rye Bread
Christy's Christmas Trees
Whole Wheat Soda Bread
Orange Bubble Loaf
Squaw Bread

SNACKING BREADS

San Diego Sunshine Bread
Herb Bread
Anne and Bill's Apple Oatmeal Bread
    with Raisins
Sweet Lelani Bread
Jalapeño Cheese Bread
Jim's Maple Walnut Bread
Linda's Lemon Bread
Jana's Seed and Nut Bread
Tomato Bread
Squaw Bread

Whole Wheat Cinnamon Raisin Bread
Dawn's Vanilla Raisin Bread
Sweet Milk Bread
Oatmeal Bread
Dennis's Multigrain Bread
Sour Rye Bread
Country Rye Bread Sticks
Midnight Sun Bread
Marmalade and Oats Bread
Max's Clogging Bread

GIFT BREADS

San Diego Sunshine Bread
Jim's Cinnamon Rolls
DeDe's Buttermilk Bread
Anne and Bill's Apple Oatmeal Bread
    with Raisins
Sweet Lelani Bread
Whole Wheat Hamburger and Hot
    Dog Buns
Jalapeño Cheese Bread
Jim's Maple Walnut Bread
Lois's Country Crunch Bread
Linda's Lemon Bread
L & L Bakers' Dill Bread
Tomato Bread
Squaw Bread
Sally Lunn Bread

Jana's Seed and Nut Bread
French Bread Extraordinaire!
Whole Wheat Cinnamon Raisin Bread
Dawn's Vanilla Raisin Bread
Sweet Milk Bread
Oatmeal Bread
Dennis's Multigrain Bread
Sour Rye Bread
Country Rye Bread Sticks
Christy's Christmas Trees
Midnight Sun Bread
Black Forest Pumpernickel
Marmalade and Oats Bread
Egg Bread
Max's Clogging Bread

DINNER PARTY BREADS

Herb Bread
Jalapeño Cheese Bread
Lois's Country Crunch Bread

Linda's Lemon Bread
Jana's Seed and Nut Bread
Lorraine's Buttermilk Rye Bread

Tomato Bread
Butterhorn Rolls
Caraway Rye Pan Rolls
Chicken Broccoli Pockets
Herb Rolls
Ann's Bierocks
Shareen's Whole Wheat Pizza
    Crust
Shayna's Vegan Burgers
Quaker Multigrain Bread
French Bread Extraordinaire!

Buttermilk Honey Bran Bread
L & L Bakers' Dill Bread
Oatmeal Bread
Sour Rye Bread
Ham and Pepper Cheese Bread
Country Rye Bread Sticks
San Francisco Sourdough Bread
Black Forest Pumpernickel
Honey Wheat Rolls
Garlic Cheese Rolls
Max's Clogging Bread

STUFFING/CROUTONS/BREAD CRUMBS

Herb Bread
Jalapeño Cheese Bread
Lois's Country Crunch Bread
Linda's Lemon Bread
Quaker Multigrain Bread
L & L Bakers' Dill Bread
Michael's Onion Rye Bread
Tomato Bread

Buttermilk Honey Bran Bread
Applesauce Rye Bread
Oatmeal Bread
Dennis's Multigrain Bread
Sour Rye Bread
San Francisco Sourdough Bread
Black Forest Pumpernickel
Egg Bread

MOST AROMATIC BREADS

San Diego Sunshine Bread
Herb Bread
Jalapeño Cheese Bread
Linda's Lemon Bread
Michael's Onion Rye Bread
Garlic Cheese Rolls

Whole Wheat Cinnamon Raisin
    Bread
Dawn's Vanilla Raisin Bread
L & L Bakers' Dill Bread
Tomato Bread
Max's Clogging Bread

BREADS THAT CAN BE BAKED ON THE DELAYED TIMER

San Diego Sunshine Bread
Anne and Bill's Apple Oatmeal
    Bread with Raisins
Heavenly Whole Wheat
    Bread

Black Forest Pumpernickel
Lois's Country Crunch Bread
Applesauce Rye Bread
Anadama Bread
Michael's Onion Rye

7
Sources

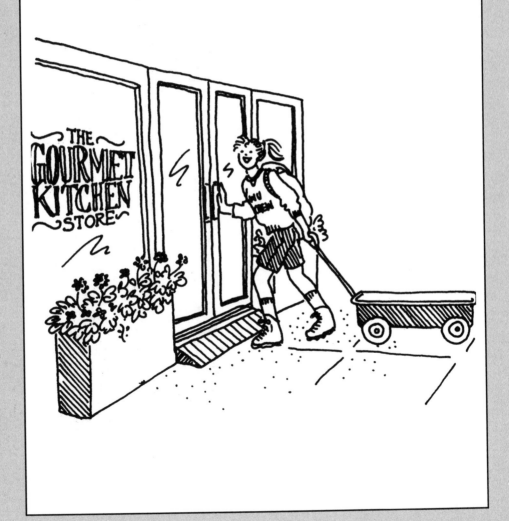

Bob's Red Mill
Natural Foods, Inc.
5209 S.E. International Way
Milwaukie, OR 97222
1-800-553-2258

A wide variety of specialty grains, cereals, and flours including stone-ground whole wheat bread flour, wheat berries for hand grinding, lecithin, whey, diastatic malt, xanthan gum, and gluten-free flours (Catalog)

Ener-G Foods, Inc.
P.O. Box 84487
Seattle, WA 98124-5787
1-800-331-5222 (outside WA)

Dietetic specialty foods such as soyquik (replaces instant nonfat dry milk), egg replacer, gluten-free flours, wheat-free and gluten-free bread machine mixes, methocel, xanthan gum, guar gum (Catalog)

The Gluten-Free Pantry
P.O. Box 840
Glastonbury, CT 06033-0840
1-860-633-3826 (customer service)
1-800-291-8386 (orders and catalog requests)
Web site: www.glutenfree.com

Gluten and wheat-free bread mixes for the bread machine and oven baking. Bread machines that work well with gluten-free flours (Catalog)

Jaffe Bros
P.O. Box 636-Z
Valley Center, CA 92082-0636
1-619-749-1133

Flours, grains, dried fruits, nuts, seeds, wheat and rye berries, hulled barley (Catalog)

King Arthur Flour
RR2, Box 56
Norwich, VT 05055
1-800-827-6836 (for orders)
1-800-777-4434 (for catalogs)

Various flours including white whole wheat flour, diastatic malt, xanthan gum, gluten-free flours, plastic bread bags for large loaves and baguettes, caramel coloring for dark rye breads, Lora Brody's sourdough bread enhancer, baking stones and peels, La Cloche, baguette pans, cookbooks (Catalog)

Miss Roben's Dietary Foods
P.O. Box 1434
Frederick, MD 21702
1-800-891-0083

Gluten-free bread mixes (Catalog)

Montana Flour and Grains
P.O. Box 517
Ft. Benton, MT 59442
1-406-622-5436

High-quality organic flour and grains. Call for information

Saco Foods
1-800-373-7226
SacoFoods@aol.com

Powdered buttermilk

Sourdoughs International, Inc.
P.O. Box 670
Cascade, ID 83611
1-208-382-4828
Web site: www.cyberhighway.net/~sourdo/

Sourdough cultures from places such as the Yukon, San Francisco, Russia, France, Austria, Egypt, Bahrain, and Saudi Arabia. They also publish a sourdough newsletter.

Universal Foods Corporation
433 East Michigan Street
P.O. Box 737
Milwaukee, WI 53201
1-800-445-4746
Web site: www.redstaryeast.com

Red Star active dry yeast, quick-rise yeast, instant yeast in bulk packages, dough conditioner, natural bread fortifier, vital gluten blend, flavor enhancer, quick bread baking powder

Walnut Acres
Penns Creek, PA 17862
1-800-433-3998

Organic flours, grains, cereals, dried fruits, nuts, herbs, and spices (Catalog)

Apropo Enterprises
10464 Clairemont Mesa Blvd. #217
San Diego, CA 92124
1-619-268-7887
Web Site: www.giftbagz.com

BakerBagz specialty gift bags for breads, clear bags with festive designs for all occasions, raffia ribbon included

The Bread Baker's Digest
List owners: Jeff and Reggie Dwork
E-mail: reggie@reggie.com

This mailing list is for discussion and recipe exchange of hand- and machine-made breads. To subscribe, send a message to <bread-bakers-request@lists.best.com> In the body put these two lines (lower case, left justified):
subscribe
end

Chef's Catalog
3215 Commercial Avenue
Northbrook, IL 60062-1900
1-800-338-3232

Professional restaurant equipment for the home chef, bread machines, French bread pans, kitchen towels, knives, necklace timer (Catalog)

K-Tec
420 North Geneva Road
Lindon, UT 84042
1-800-748-5400
Web site: www.k-tecusa.com

Bread mixes, grain mills, and baking supplies

Miles Kimball
41 East Eighth Avenue
Oshkosh, WI 54906-0002

Personalized paper bread bags and expandable plastic bread boxes (Catalog)

Wanda's Nature Farm Foods
850 NBC Center
Lincoln, NE 68508
1-800-222-FARM
E-mail: naturefarm@aol.com

Expandable bread boxes, bread machine mixes, including pizza, focaccia, bagel, and pretzel mixes (Catalog)

Bailey, Janet. *Keeping Food Fresh.* New York: Harper & Row, 1989.

Beard, James. *Beard on Bread.* New York: Ballantine Books, 1973.

Better Homes and Gardens. *Complete Guide to Food and Cooking.* Des Moines, IA: Meredith Corp., 1991.

Brody, Jane. *Jane Brody's Good Food Book.* New York: W. W. Norton & Co., 1985.

———. *Jane Brody's Nutrition Book.* New York: W. W. Norton & Co., 1981.

———. *The New York Times Guide to Personal Health.* New York: Times Books, 1982.

Clayton, Jr., Bernard. *Bernard Clayton's New Complete Book of Breads.* New York: Simon & Schuster, 1987.

Dworkin, Floss, and Stan Dworkin. *Bake Your Own Bread.* New York: Plume, 1987.

Eckhardt, Linda West, and Diana Collingwood Butts. *Bread in Half the Time.* New York: Crown Publishers, 1991.

Hittner, Patricia. "The New Food Additives: Can They Really Deliver Flavor Without Guilt?" *Better Homes and Gardens,* April 1992.

Jones, Judith, and Evan Jones. *The Book of Bread.* New York: Harper & Row, 1982.

Kilham, Christopher S. *The Bread and Circus Whole Food Bible.* Reading, MA: Addison-Wesley Publishing Co., 1991.

Manning, Elise W. *Farm Journal's Complete Home Baking Book.* Garden City, NY: Doubleday & Co., 1979.

Mindell, Earl. *Vitamin Bible.* New York: Warner Books, 1979.

McGee, Harold. *On Food and Cooking: The Science and Lore of the Kitchen.* New York: Collier Books, 1984.

Moore, Ken. *Bread Baking: Problems and Their Solutions.* Ukiah, CA: Moore Publishing, 1991.

Moore, Marilyn M. *The Wooden Spoon Bread Book.* New York: The Atlantic Monthly Press, 1987.

Ojakangas, Beatrice. *Great Whole-Grain Breads.* New York: Dutton, 1984.

Pappas, Lou Seibert. *Bread Baking.* San Leandro, CA: Bristol Publishing, 1992.

"Quinoa, the Healthful Grain." *Better Homes and Gardens,* December 1992.

Robertson, Laurel. *The Laurel's Kitchen Bread Book.* New York: Random House, 1984.

Rombauer, Irma S., and Marion Rombauer Becker. *Joy of Cooking.* New York: Bobbs-Merrill Co., 1975.

Index

You can obtain additional copies of this book, or the authors' best-selling cookbook *Bread Machine Magic,* at your local bookseller, or by using the coupon below.

ORDER FORM

Please send me the following books:

_____ copies of *The Bread Machine Magic Book of Helpful Hints*
    (ISBN 0-312-24123-2 $11.95)
_____ copies of *Bread Machine Magic*
    (ISBN 0-312-06914-6 $11.95)
_____ copies of *More Bread Machine Magic*
    (ISBN 0-312-16935-3 $11.95)

Enclosed is a check or money order, payable to Publishers Book & Audio, in the amount of $ _____ (please include shipping and handling charges of $3.00 for the first book, and $1.00 for each additional book).

Send books to: Name _____

                  Address _____

                  _____

                  _____

Send this coupon and your payment to: Publishers Book & Audio, P.O. Box 070059, Staten Island, New York 10307. Please allow four to six weeks for delivery.

For bulk orders (10 or more copies), contact St. Martin's Press, Special Markets Division, 175 Fifth Avenue, New York, NY 10010. Or call, toll free, 1-800-221-7945, extension #645, 636, 628, or 662.